Lively Bible Lessons
for Kindergarten

Edited by Beth Rowland

Loveland, Colorado

Credits
Edited by Beth Rowland
Cover designed by Jean Bruns
Interior designed by Dori Walker
Illustrations by Jan Knudson

Unless otherwise noted, Scriptures are quoted from **The Everyday Bible, New Century Version**, copyright © 1987, 1988 Word Publishing, Dallas, Texas 75039. Used by permission.

Library of Congress Cataloging-in-Publication Data
Lively Bible lessons for kindergarten / edited by Beth Rowland.
    p.   cm.
  ISBN 1-55945-097-5
  1. Christian education of children. 2. Bible crafts.
 I. Rowland, Beth. II. Group Books (Firm)
 BV1475.8.L58 1992
 268'.432—dc20   92-16301
                                                  CIP

Printed in the United States of America.

CONTENTS

Part 3: A Lively Look at My Relationships

Part 4: A Lively Look at Celebrations

INTRODUCTION

Welcome to a resource filled with lively, active Bible lessons for kindergartners. Here are fun meetings that'll hold your kids' attention and teach self-esteem-building, friendship-boosting, faith-developing topics.

In *Lively Bible Lessons for Kindergarten*, Sunday school teachers, vacation Bible school teachers, after-school program directors and any leader of kindergartners will find 20 simple-to-follow lessons that combine lively learning, colorful art projects and scrumptious snacks.

The book is divided into these four parts:

● **Part 1: A Lively Look at My Faith**—Children are interested in God, the church and their developing faith. Faith-building topics include Creation, the Bible, Jesus as our friend and the church family.

● **Part 2: A Lively Look at Myself**—Children are growing and changing daily. This section covers topics that help kids with prayer, fear, loneliness, obedience and spreading God's light.

● **Part 3: A Lively Look at My Relationships**—This section helps children look past themselves to others. Topics include cooperation, sharing, saying "I'm sorry" and kindness.

● **Part 4: A Lively Look at Celebrations**—People of all ages love to celebrate special occasions. This section offers Bible lessons for birthdays, Valentine's Day, Easter, Thanksgiving and Christmas.

THE LIVELY BIBLE LESSONS

The lessons in *Lively Bible Lessons for Kindergarten* each contain at least seven activities. Each activity lasts no longer than 12 minutes. The activities are fast-paced and fun for children with short attention spans. Each lesson is divided into the following elements:

● **Introduction**—One or two paragraphs that give an overview of the lesson's topic.

● **A Powerful Purpose**—A short statement of the lesson's objective, telling you what children will learn.

● **A Look at the Lesson**—An outline including activity titles and estimated completion times. These times may vary depending on your class size.

● **A Sprinkling of Supplies**—A list of all items you'll need for the lesson.

● **The Lively Lesson**—Quick, active, reflective, scripture-based activities. Lessons start with an opening experience to set the mood for the upcoming lesson. Kids experience the topics through active learning using their senses of hearing, seeing, smelling, tasting and feeling.

Lessons include participation Bible stories, action-packed rhymes, songs to familiar tunes, art projects and snacks.

● **Handouts**—All necessary handouts are included. They're easy to use and you have permission to photocopy them for local church use.

Enjoy *Lively Bible Lessons for Kindergarten*. Use and adapt the Bible lessons for any size group. Watch kids develop self-esteem, meet new friends and grow in their faith. And have fun teaching topics in an active, lively and meaningful way!

PART 1:
A LIVELY LOOK
AT MY FAITH

GOD MADE EVERYTHING

Have you ever found yourself marveling at God's creation? For most kindergarten children, every day is filled with that kind of joy and wonder. There is a whole world opening up for them to explore and marvel at.

As a teacher you're in the perfect position to help children use their ever-increasing skills to discover and learn more about God, whose love is the source of all life. Use this lesson to help your kindergartners discover the variety of things God's created and learn to enjoy and celebrate the wonderful gift of creation.

A POWERFUL PURPOSE

Kindergartners will use their developing skills to recognize and celebrate the creation of a mighty and loving God.

A LOOK AT THE LESSON

1. Seedy Things (8 to 10 minutes)
2. Things God Made (up to 5 minutes)
3. It Only Took 7 Days (8 to 10 minutes)
4. God's Zoo (up to 5 minutes)
5. Climb a Mountain, Cross a Sea (8 to 12 minutes)
6. Creation Mix (up to 5 minutes)
7. Saying Thank You (up to 5 minutes)

A SPRINKLING OF SUPPLIES

Gather an assortment of seeds, grains, gravel, sand, cotton, broken-up pine cones and other natural materials. You'll also need construction paper, glue, jar lids or wax paper, cotton swabs, crayons, balloons, magazine pictures, a marker, a Bible, a glue stick, a large bowl, an assortment of animal-shaped crackers and candies, paper cups and juice.

THE LIVELY LESSON

1. Seedy Things

(You'll need an assortment of seeds, grains, gravel, sand, cotton, broken-up pine cones and other natural materials. You'll also need construction paper, glue, jar lids or wax paper, cotton swabs and crayons.)

As you welcome the children, ask them to make collages by gluing the natural materials onto the construction paper. With this age, it works best to provide small puddles of glue in jar lids or on wax paper. Show them how to use their cotton swabs to paint a small area of their papers with glue and then press or sprinkle the natural materials onto the glue.

As the children work, ask:
● **What are you gluing to your paper?**
● **Where did that material come from?**
● **What do we use that material for?**

Discuss how the materials look and feel. As children are working, write each child's name on his or her picture or have kids write their own names on their pictures. When the kids are finished, set the pictures aside to dry.

Ask:

● **Who creates seeds, sand and pine cones?**

● **Why does God make so many wonderful things?**

2. Things God Made

Gather children in an open area and sit in a circle.

Play this categories-type game to explore the variety in God's creation. Have kids sit cross-legged and keep up this four-beat rhythm: slap thighs twice, then clap hands twice. Practice for a while until kids are comfortable with the "slap, slap, clap, clap" beat. Then go around the circle and have the kids complete this sentence, one at a time, while keeping up the rhythm: "God made..." It's a good idea if you start off with an example such as "God made mountains."

Don't feel you need to have a response with each rhythm sequence. Feel free to give kids time to think of a response. Remember that ultimately everything stems from God's creation so there won't be any wrong answers!

Ask:

● **What would the world be like if God hadn't created these things?** You may want to ask what the world would be like without specific creations that class members said during the game.

Say: **I'm thankful that we live in a world with mountains, sunshine and flowers. God has made many things for us to enjoy.**

3. It Only Took 7 Days

(Before class blow up seven balloons and cut out several magazine pictures that illustrate what was created each day. There's a list of scripture references and possible pictures for each day of Creation below. You'll also need a marker, a Bible and a glue stick. Have extra balloons available in case any pop.)

Say: **The Bible tells us about the time long, long ago when God created the world.**

Scatter the magazine pictures in the middle of the circle of kids. As you read the verses that correspond with each day of Creation, write the number of the day on a blown-up balloon with a marker. Tell kids to look at the pictures and find those that show what happened during that day while you read the verses. Have anyone who finds a picture paste it to the balloon with a glue stick. After each picture is pasted onto the balloon, ask the children to say with you: **And God said, "That's good."**

Read these verses: *Purple*

Day One: Genesis 1:1, 3, 5 (light, daytime, nighttime)

Day Two: Genesis 1:7-8 (sky) *Blue*

Day Three: Genesis 1:9-11, 13 (earth, *Green*, seas, plants)

Day Four: Genesis 1:16-17, 19 (sun, *Yellow* moon, stars)

Day Five: Genesis 1:20, 23 (birds, *pink* fish)

Day Six: Genesis 1:24, 26, 31 (animals, humans)

Day Seven: Genesis 2:1-3 (rest)

Put the balloons aside to use in the last activity.

4. God's Zoo

Say: **Some of my favorite things that God created are the animals! Let's all pretend we're big bears and walk around the room.**

After you choose the first few animals, ask different children to pretend to be their favorites while the rest of the class guesses which animal is being portrayed.

Calm children down before going on to the next activity by choosing one or two quiet animals such as turtles or snakes for them to imitate.

5. Climb a Mountain, Cross a Sea

In this game of Follow the Leader, use whatever is in your room, such as chairs and tables, to make this an exciting journey.

Say: **Let's pretend we're explorers on a journey to find God's creation.**

Have kids follow you on the journey and imitate your actions. Lead the class through the adventures listed below, pausing to act each one out.

Say: **One day, a group of explorers decided to search the world to find God's creation. So they made a lunch** (pause), **packed their bags** (pause), **waved goodbye to their moms and dads** (pause) **and took the path that led to the wilderness** (march around the room), **where they**

found a meadow of wildflowers (talk about the colors, smell the fragrance of the flowers),

climbed a tall, steep mountain (climb up the mountain, dodge a landslide, find shelter in a tunnel when a storm blows up, listen to the thunder, see the flash of lightning),

reached the top of the mountain (look down at the clouds and the birds, pause to eat lunch, scramble up trees to get away from a bear that's come to eat their lunches),

rolled down the other side of the mountain,

landed on a sandy shore (feel the warmth of the sun on the sand, build a sand castle),

sailed across an ocean (listen to the waves crash on the shore, climb into a boat, see the wind fill the sails, speed over the ocean to the sandy shore on the other side of the ocean),

and watched a sunset (after a long day's journey, sit on the sand and watch the sun set).

Ask:

● **What did we find on our journey that's part of God's creation?**

Say: **God's creation is all around us. We celebrate God's creation whenever we take time to enjoy it. Let's celebrate another of God's creations by eating a snack.**

6. Creation Mix

(In a large bowl, make Creation Mix out of animal-shaped crackers and candies such as Teddy Grahams, Dinosaur Grrrahams, animal crackers and Gummi Bears. You'll also need small paper cups and juice.)

Let kids fill paper cups with the Creation Mix. Serve juice, too. Talk about each kid's favorite part of God's creation as everyone munches on the snack.

7. Saying Thank You

Scatter the Creation balloons around the room for this prayer activity. Have all the children gather around the balloon for Day One. Thank God for that day's creations by having kids complete this sentence prayer: "Thank you, God, for..." Then move the class to the balloon for Day Two. Keep going until you've thanked God for all of creation.

by Eric Sandras

GOD'S SPECIAL BOOK

With all the competition for children's attention these days, getting them interested in reading can be a challenge. But even in our TV and video world, kindergartners still find books exciting.

As a teacher you have the opportunity to introduce children to the Bible before they can read. Why? Because a child doesn't have to be able to read to enjoy a good book. All they need is their God-given imagination and your positive encouragement.

A POWERFUL PURPOSE

Children will learn that the Bible is God's special book and that it was written for them.

A LOOK AT THE LESSON

1. Words Say A Lot (up to 5 minutes)
2. What's in the Bible? (10 to 12 minutes)
3. Story Time (5 to 10 minutes)
4. Picture This (5 to 10 minutes)
5. What's It Mean? (5 to 10 minutes)
6. Sweet Words (up to 5 minutes)
7. It's the Book for Me (up to 5 minutes)

A SPRINKLING OF SUPPLIES

Gather a Bible and a paper bag filled with a personal letter, a storybook, a poem, a sheet of music and an instruction manual. You'll also need crayons, scissors, tape, a paper plate, a ruler, a photocopy of the "Jeremiah the Puppet" handout, magazine pictures that show love, glue, construction paper, a hole punch, yarn, a marker, bread, honey in squeeze bottles, milk, napkins and paper cups.

THE LIVELY LESSON

1. Words Say A Lot

Gather the children and sit down in an open area of the room. Ask:

● **How many of you like books?**
● **What do you like about books?**
Say: **It's fun to cuddle with moms and dads and read books together. Sometimes it's nice to read and look at books all by ourselves. Books can take us on many adventures just by using words and pictures. Let's see what words can do.**

Have kids stand and act out these words with you. Say:

Some words are happy like smile, skip and dance.

Some words are sad like cry, shuffle and pout.

Some words are noisy like clap, pop and stomp.

Some words are jumpy like hop, bounce and leap.

Some words are fun like wiggle, twirl and giggle.

And some words are quiet like whisper, tiptoe and listen.

Have kids sit in a circle. Ask:

● **What kinds of words do you like best?**

● **What kinds of books do you like best?**

Say: **Today we're going to find out about a book written just for you. It's called the Bible.**

2. What's in the Bible?

(You'll need a Bible and a paper bag filled with a personal letter, a storybook, a poem, a sheet of music and an instruction manual such as one from a VCR. Be sure to get permission if you choose to photocopy a copyright poem or piece of music.)

Show kids the Bible and say: **The Bible looks like an ordinary book, but it's not. It's filled with many different kinds of books.**

Have volunteers reach into the paper bag and pull out the items one at a time. As each item is pulled out, ask kids if they know which part of the Bible is like the item that's been pulled out of the paper bag. If they don't know, use these explanations to show them how the Bible is like the item.

The personal letter: Explain that the letter was written to share news because the writer cares about the person the letter was written to. Tell kids the Bible has many letters in it. Explain that the whole Bible is a letter from God to people all over the world.

The storybook: Tell kids the Bible is full of exciting stories such as the story about David and Goliath. Ask children to name stories they know from the Bible.

The poem: Kindergartners may be unfamiliar with poems, especially written ones. Read the poem, and tell kids that in Bible times, people wrote poems to tell God how they felt and to praise God. Tell them writing poems also made it easier for the people to remember what had been written. The people could memorize the poems and know important things about God.

The sheet of music: Tell kids the Bible has many songs in it. Many of them were written to praise God.

The instruction manual: Tell kids the Bible gives us instructions on how to follow God. The Bible helps us make good choices so we can make God happy.

After all the items have been chosen and explained, say: **I like the stories that are in the Bible. Listen to this story about a man who wrote part of the Bible.**

3. Story Time

(You'll need crayons, scissors, tape, a paper plate, a ruler, the puppet face from the "Jeremiah the Puppet" handout and a Bible. Make the Jeremiah puppet before class using the instructions on the handout.)

Use the puppet to tell Jeremiah's story. Open the Bible to the first chapter of Jeremiah so kids can see where the story comes from when the puppet shows it to them.

Say: **My name is Jeremiah. I lived in a country called Judah a long time before Jesus was born. In those days God was unhappy with the way people were living. People didn't obey God, and it made God sad.**

One day God said to me, "Jeremiah, before you were born, I decided to give you a very special job. I decided to send you as a messenger to my people."

I said to God, "I don't know how to be a messenger. I'm not very good at speaking. Besides, I'm just a young boy. What if I mess up?"

God answered, "Don't worry. You don't need to be scared. Never

say that you're too young. Since I have asked you to do this for me, I will protect you and make you strong."

Then I felt better because I knew that God is strong enough to take care of me.

God said, "Your job is to go everywhere I send you and tell the people everything I tell you to say."

God wanted someone to warn people about doing bad things. God knows that doing bad things can hurt us. It was my job to warn everyone.

So that's what I did. I told the people to stop doing wrong and to obey God. Some people listened and that made God glad. But many people didn't listen and that made God sad.

Then God told me to write down his words. The book is named after me and it's in the Bible. I even put this story in my book. See, it's right here at the very beginning of the book.

4. Picture This

(Provide an assortment of magazine pictures that show love, glue and construction paper folded in half with two holes punched $1/4$ inch in from the crease and 2 inches from the top and bottom. You'll also need yarn.)

Form groups of four. Give each group one folded sheet of construction paper. Have each child choose one picture to glue onto one page of their "book."

Say: **We're making a book about love, so make sure you choose a picture that makes you think of love.** Tell the children to save room on the pages for words.

As children finish, gather their books together one on top of the other so the holes line up. Put a strand of yarn through the holes and tie it to bind the books together to make one book.

CONSTRUCTION PAPER BOOK

Say: **This is how the Bible was written. With God's help, many people wrote books that were all put together to make one big book—the Bible.**

5. What's It Mean?

(You'll need a marker.)

Say: **We need to put some words in our book. Let's decide what some of the pages of our book say about love.**

Hold up one page at a time and ask the children to tell you what to write. Explain that God helped the writers of the Bible know what to say (like the children with this book), and the writers put down the words (like you're doing.) As time allows, choose one or two pictures from each small book and write a couple of sentences about each. Write words the children suggest.

When finished, say: **Now we've made our own special book about love. The Bible is God's special book about love, and God gave it to us.**

6. Sweet Words

(You'll need bread, honey in squeeze bottles, milk, napkins and paper cups. If there isn't a sink close by, have warm, wet washcloths available to clean sticky hands.)

Say: **The Bible tells us that pleasant words are like honey, making people happy and healthy. The Bible is full of pleasant words, so let's eat some honey on our bread and enjoy the sweet gift God has given us.**

Serve the treats.

7. It's the Book for Me

(You'll need a Bible.)

Gather kids in a circle. Pass the Bible around the circle as everyone sings "The B-I-B-L-E," "Jesus Loves Me" or some other song about the Bible. When you get to the end of the song, have the child who is holding the Bible complete this sentence prayer: "Thank you, God, for putting _____ in the Bible." For example, the child might say, "Thank you, God, for putting stories in the Bible." Then have children continue to pass the Bible as they sing the song again. Continue until all the children have a chance to pray.

Children like repetition. But if you have more than 10 kids in your class, keep them interested in this activity by having several children pray at the end of the song.

by Eric Sandras

JEREMIAH THE PUPPET

Photocopy and color this face, cut it out and tape it onto a paper plate. Tape a ruler to the back of the paper plate.

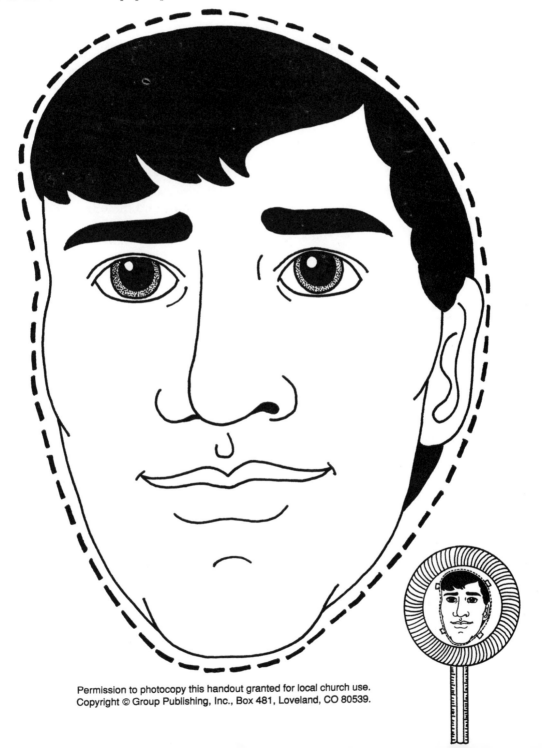

My Forever Friend

Kindergartners need to learn how important a friendship with Jesus is to their lives. They're developing relationships with other children and have probably experienced love, hurt and rejection among their friends. Through this lesson kindergartners will learn that Jesus is a friend who'll always be there for them, no matter what the circumstance.

A POWERFUL PURPOSE

Through this lesson children will learn that Jesus is their friend.

A LOOK AT THE LESSON

1. The Friendship Sheet (8 to 10 minutes)
2. Friendly Wrap-Up (5 to 10 minutes)
3. Jesus Is a Friend to Children (up to 5 minutes)
4. I'm a Friend to Jesus (up to 5 minutes)
5. I See Jesus in Others (8 to 10 minutes)
6. Hug Snacks (up to 5 minutes)
7. We're All Friends (5 to 10 minutes)
8. Thanks for Friendship (up to 5 minutes)

A SPRINKLING OF SUPPLIES

Gather a white sheet, markers, Bible, fruit Roll-Up snacks, fruit slices and cheese strips.

THE LIVELY LESSON

1. The Friendship Sheet

(You'll need a white sheet and markers.)

Spread out the white sheet on the floor. If your floor is carpeted, join tables together and spread the sheet on top of them. Have the children gather around the edges of the sheet. Invite children to draw pictures of friends and of things they do with their friends. Make sure they leave plenty of space in the center of the sheet. When they are finished, have the children tell the kids sitting on either side of them about their pictures.

Say: **Today we'll talk about someone who wants to be your best friend. His name is Jesus.**

In the center of the sheet, draw a picture of Jesus or have a child draw a picture of Jesus.

This sheet will be used throughout the lesson. After class, you can keep the sheet to give kids "Jesus Hugs" whenever they need to feel Jesus' love. You can hang the sheet in your room as a reminder of Jesus' friendship. Or you can arrange to hang it in your sanctuary for a worship service.

2. Friendly Wrap-Up

(You'll need the sheet.)
Ask:
● **Why is it good to have friends?**
● **Have you ever had a friend**

who did something mean to you?

● Have you ever wished for a friend when you didn't have one?

Say: **God gives us friends for lots of reasons. We can have fun together. We can help each other. And friends keep us from being lonely. But sometimes friends can hurt us. We can get in arguments and fight, even though we're really good friends. Jesus is a friend who will never hurt us. He loves us and will always do what's best for us.**

Have kids each wrap themselves up in the sheet and talk about a time when they needed a friend. A child might say, "I needed a friend when we moved here, and I didn't have anyone to play with." While the child is still wrapped in the sheet, say to him or her: **Jesus will be your friend.**

3. Jesus Is a Friend to Children

(You'll need a Bible.)

Gather kids in a circle. Open the Bible to Matthew 19:13-15. Tell this story: **Jesus had been with the people for a long time. He healed them. And he taught them. Crowds of people followed him as he went from place to place telling them God loved them.**

Some parents brought their children to Jesus so Jesus could pray for them. But the men that helped Jesus told the parents to leave and take their children away from Jesus.

But Jesus said, "Let the children come to me. God's kingdom belongs to people who are like children."

Then Jesus gathered the children into his arms and he prayed for them.

4. I'm a Friend to Jesus

(You'll need markers and the sheet.)

Say: **We drew all our friendship pictures far away from Jesus. Let's draw pictures of ourselves close to Jesus to show that we want to be friends with him.**

Have children draw pictures of themselves close to the picture of Jesus in the middle of the sheet.

5. I See Jesus in Others

Ask:

● **What kinds of things do friends do together?**

● **Since we're friends with Jesus, what kinds of things can we do with him?**

Say: **Jesus lives in heaven, so it's hard to do some kinds of friendly things with him, like playing ball or eating a snack. But it's easy to do other things with Jesus. We can talk to Jesus any time and know he listens to us. The Bible also says that any time we do something nice for people, we're really doing something nice for Jesus.**

Let's do some friendly things for each other to show how much we want to be friends with Jesus.

Have kids do or pretend to do these friendly things. Say:

Find a friend and shake his or her hand.

Find another friend and share a snack.

Find another friend and share a secret.

Find another friend and give him or her a drink.

Find another friend and play a game of catch.

Find another friend and bandage an "owie."

Find another friend and share a hug.

Say: **Jesus sure has a lot of good friends here.**

6. Hug Snacks

(You'll need fruit Roll-Up snacks, sliced fruit such as apples and pears, and strips of cheese.)

As a snack serve "Hugs From Jesus." Have kids roll up fruit slices and cheese strips in a fruit Roll-Up snack. Tell kids to pretend that Jesus is the fruit Roll-Up and they are the fruit and cheese. Say: **Jesus wants to roll you up in his love and give you a great big hug.**

7. We're All Friends

(You'll need the sheet and a marker.)

Draw a happy face on the edge of the sheet. Have kids stand around the sheet and hold it at waist level. Sing a song such as "Jesus Loves Me" or the "Jesus is a friend" verse of the song "Ah, La, La, La." Both songs are in *The Group Songbook* (Group Books).

While you sing, have the kids turn the sheet around the group by passing it hand to hand. At the end of the song, whoever is closest to the happy face crawls under the sheet. The rest of the kids should make the sheet billow up and settle gently on the child so that it forms an "air tent." Say: **Jesus is your friend and we're your friends, too.** Continue until everyone has a chance to be under the sheet.

8. Thanks for Friendship

Have everyone sit on their knees while holding on to the sheet. Billow the sheet up one last time and have everyone scurry under the sheet before it falls. As the sheet falls, pray: **Thank you, Jesus, for being such a good friend to us. Help us to be friends with you and with each other. Amen.**

by Janel Kauffman

GOD'S FAMILY

"There's our church!" Children hear adults refer to the church building as the church so often that it's sometimes difficult for them to understand that the "church" is really people.

An entertaining finger play we did as children even reinforced this: "Here's the church, here's the steeple, open the door and here are the people."

Children need to understand that people are the building blocks of the church. Use this lesson to help them see they are part of God's family.

A POWERFUL PURPOSE

Children will learn that the church is the family of God.

A LOOK AT THE LESSON

1. Dressing Up (8 to 10 minutes)
2. Church-Building (up to
   5 minutes)
3. A Look at the Church (5 to
   10 minutes)
4. Multiplication (5 to 10 minutes)
5. The Church at Work (5 to
   10 minutes)
6. Sing-Along (up to 5 minutes)
7. Jelly Belly (up to 5 minutes)
8. Thanks for the Church (up to
   5 minutes)

A SPRINKLING OF SUPPLIES

Gather dress-up clothes, a home center, toy people figures, a large sheet of paper, scissors, a Bible, photocopies of the "Church Work" handout, wax paper, tape, colored glue and jelly beans.

THE LIVELY LESSON

1. Dressing Up

(You'll need a box of family dress-up clothes and a home center. If your classroom doesn't have a home center, bring in some plastic dishes and old pots and pans. A classroom table can become a dining room table. Paint four circles on a piece of plywood to make a stove. A plastic tub makes a great sink.)

As children arrive, lead them to the box of clothing. Encourage them to dress like family members. Some kids can be moms and dads, some can be grandparents and some can be babies. Give the kids several minutes to play house.

Afterward, have them sit in a circle on the floor. Have children tell you about their families. Be sensitive to kids whose families don't include a mom or a dad or brothers or sisters. Reassure kids by telling them that all families are different.

Ask:
● **What's your favorite part of being a family?**
● **How do people in your family take care of each other?**
● **What does your family do when they're happy?**

● **How do you take care of each other when you're sad or hurt?**

Say: **It feels good to be part of a family, because family members love each other and take care of each other. Today we're going to talk about God's family—the church. When God's family comes to this building, we learn about God and do things that show how happy we are that he is the head of our family.**

2. Church-Building

(You'll need a box of toy people figures such as Weebles, Fisher-Price or Lego people.)

Tell the kids that they're going to build a church. Give children the box of toy people. You may notice some confusion. If so, play with the children and help choose one figure to be the pastor, several to be teachers, several to be people who serve others as ushers, cooks and custodians, several to be people who tell others about Jesus, several to be people learning about Jesus, and so on.

3. A Look at the Church

Take children to look at the outside of your church, and explain to children that the church is not only a building—the church is God's family. Then take children on a silent walk through the inside of the church. Tell them to look for people who are part of the church family.

When you get back to your classroom, ask:

● **Who did you see who's in God's family?**

● **What do those people do at the church?**

Ask them which type of person in the church they'd like to be, such as someone in the choir, a Sunday school teacher, the person who collects the offering or the pastor.

4. Multiplication

(You'll need a large sheet of paper, scissors and a Bible.)

Gather children in a circle on the floor. Say: **When Jesus started the family of God, he started with the disciples—his closest friends. Let's find out what happened after Jesus' death and resurrection.**

Tell the story below, or have an adult volunteer tell the story, while you do this paper-cutting activity. You can also tape-record the story to play as you cut the paper people.

Fold a large sheet of paper in half, short end to short end. Then fold it in half again in the same direction. Fold the paper several times— the more times the better. Cut a

PAPER PEOPLE

people figure out of the folded paper. The arms and legs on both edges should touch the folds. Don't cut through the folds where the arms and legs touch them. When you finish your story and paper cutting, you'll have a string of paper people.

Open the Bible to Acts 2. Tell this story as the paper people are cut: **Jesus' disciples were in Jerusalem waiting. A few days earlier, Jesus** had gone to heaven. Before he rose up into the clouds, he told the disciples to wait in Jerusalem because God was going to give them something he had promised.

The promise came true on a holiday called Pentecost. The disciples were all together when a noise like a strong wind started inside the house where they were sitting. Then they saw what looked like fire. The fire broke into flames that appeared over each person's head. The Holy Spirit came to them and they started to speak in different languages.

There were lots of people in Jerusalem. They were celebrating the Pentecost holiday. The people came from many different countries and spoke many different languages. But because of the Holy Spirit, the disciples could speak all the languages. The disciples told everyone about the wonderful things God had done. They told the people about how much Jesus loved them and about how Jesus had died for them.

Unfold the paper people to show that many people joined together to make the church. Say: **Hundreds and hundreds of people believed what the disciples were saying. They decided they wanted to become Christians. On that very day they became Christians and started to learn about God. They also shared everything they owned. They met together to eat and learn and pray. This was the beginning of the church.**

When people become Christians, they're added to God's church. God's church is made of people. Let's look at some things God's church does.

5. The Church at Work

(You'll need the symbols from photocopies of the "Church Work" handout, scissors, wax paper, tape and Elmer's Glucolors or glue colored with food coloring.)

Show kids the cutout symbols from the "Church Work" handout. Explain what each symbol means to the church. For example, for the fellowship symbol say, "God's church gets together to encourage each other and have fun together."

Have kids each choose a symbol of the church. Then give each child a small piece of wax paper. Help children tape their symbols to their pieces of wax paper. The wax paper should cover the front of the symbol. Then encourage children to cover their symbols with different colors of glue. It's important that there aren't many holes left without glue. The more holes there are, the weaker the glue symbol.

When the glue symbols are finished, use the glue to write each child's name on the edge of his or her wax paper. Let the symbols dry until the next time you meet. When the symbols are dry, kids can peel the symbols off of the wax paper and take them home. Have kids explain to their families what their church symbols mean.

The glue symbols will stick to a smooth surface such as a mirror or a refrigerator. They come off easily and won't leave a mark.

6. Sing-Along

Say: **Let's sing a song about being part of God's family.**

Have children sing this song to the tune of "The Muffin Man."

We are part of God's great church,

**God's great church,
God's great church.
We are part of God's great church,
God's special family.**

After singing this through one time, go around the circle and replace each child's name in the place of "we." Sing the song again with each child's name. For example, sing, "Kelly's part of God's great church, God's great church, God's great church. Kelly's part of God's great church, God's special family."

7. Jelly Belly

(You'll need jelly beans.)

Say: **The church is not only a building. The church is God's people, who are called Christians. Christians are people who follow Jesus. People in the church are more important than the bricks or rocks in the buildings. Let's play a game with our snack to pretend that we're building a church of God's people.**

Give children each several jelly beans. Help them work together to construct a flat building on the table that resembles a church building. Then have them make several jelly bean people inside the church. Let them

enjoy their jelly beans. Watch small children carefully to make sure they chew their jelly beans well.

8. Thanks for the Church

Have each child pick one thing that people in the church do. Kids could pick praying, teaching, preaching, cooking, singing, eating, taking care of the babies, working in the yard or cleaning the sanctuary. Have them all silently act out their job. While they are acting, pray: **God, thank you for all the things that your family does and for letting us be part of your family. Amen.**

by Christine Yount

CHURCH WORK

Photocopy this page and cut apart the symbols. You'll need enough for each child to have one.

PART 2:
A LIVELY LOOK AT MYSELF

I Can Talk to God

The Bible contains many accounts of the impact, purpose and priority of prayer. The story of Peter's release from prison is one example. The Christians prayed earnestly for Peter's release. Yet when he appeared at the door, they were astonished.

We all need to learn that prayer is powerful. It's not always easy to realize that a magnificent and powerful God pays attention to the prayers of his people. But it's a lesson every child (and adult) needs to learn.

A POWERFUL PURPOSE

Children will discover they can talk to a God who listens.

A LOOK AT THE LESSON

1. I Can Talk to God (5 to 10 minutes)
2. Puppet Prayer (up to 5 minutes)
3. Prayer for Peter (5 to 10 minutes)
4. Prayer Paintings (5 to 10 minutes)
5. Where Can I Pray? (up to 5 minutes)
6. A Thankful Prayer (up to 5 minutes)
7. A Song About Prayer (up to 5 minutes)
8. Let's Pray (up to 5 minutes)

A SPRINKLING OF SUPPLIES

Gather two disposable cups, string, photocopies of the "Puppet Page" handout, scissors, crayons, glue or tape, Popsicle sticks, cellulose sponge, clothespins, tempera paint, small pans, paper, treats such as cookies and milk, napkins and a playground ball.

THE LIVELY LESSON

1. I Can Talk to God

(Before class, make a play telephone. Punch holes in the bottoms of two disposable cups. Connect the two cups by threading the end of a 20-foot piece of string through each hole and tying a knot.)

Show children the phone you made. Have kids experiment talking on the phone. Does it work better if they stand with the string taut or loose? What happens if the string touches something? Can they hear if they whisper? What happens if the two children on the phone speak to each other from different rooms?

Say: **Talking on the telephone is fun. But this phone doesn't work as well as a real one does.**

Have kids find a partner by grabbing the hand of someone close to them. Have them pretend to talk to each other on telephones as they answer these questions.

Ask:
● **Have you ever talked on a real telephone?**
● **Who have you talked to on the phone?**
● **What did you talk about on the phone?**

Say: **Today we're going to learn about talking to God. Talking to God is like talking on a telephone because you can't see God, just like you can't see the person you talk to on a telephone. But we know that God hears us whenever and wherever we pray.**

2. Puppet Prayer

(You'll need photocopies of the "Puppet Page" handout, scissors, crayons, glue or tape, and Popsicle sticks.)

Make enough photocopies of the puppets from the "Puppet Page" handout for each person to have one puppet. You'll need a King Herod, a Peter, an angel and a Rhoda. The rest of the class can be guards and Christians. If you have more than 12 children, make two sets of puppets. Have kids color the figures and glue or tape Popsicle sticks to the backs.

3. Prayer for Peter

Gather kids in an open area of the room. Have children act out the story with their puppets as you tell it.

Say: **King Herod was a very evil man. He didn't like Christians very much so he told his soldiers to arrest Peter and throw him in jail. The guards put chains on Peter and sat next to him so he couldn't get away. They wanted to make sure Peter stayed in jail.**

When the Christians heard that Peter was in jail, they all got together and prayed for him.

One night when Peter was sleeping, an angel came to the prison. The angel woke Peter up. The angel said, "Hurry, Peter! Get up!" The chains fell off Peter's hands and he

got up. **Then the angel said, "Get dressed, Peter, and follow me." So Peter got dressed and followed the angel. They went past the guards. When they were outside the prison, they walked down a street. Then the angel left Peter all alone.**

Peter was very thankful. He said, "God has rescued me." Then Peter hurried to the place where the Christians were and knocked on the door. The Christians were praying. When they heard the knock at the door, they sent Rhoda to see who was there. When she asked, "Who's there?" Peter said, "It's me, Peter."

Rhoda was so excited that Peter was out of prison, she forgot to open the door. She ran back to the other Christians and said, "Peter's at the door." The Christians said, "You're crazy. Peter's not here." But Rhoda said again, "Peter really is here!"

Peter had to knock on the door again. This time the Christians came to the door and they let him in. Peter said, "God rescued me from prison." The Christians were very happy that God had answered their prayers.

4. Prayer Paintings

(You'll need a cellulose sponge cut up in 1-inch pieces, clothespins, tempera paint, small pans and paper. Use the clothespins as handles for the sponges. Put tempera paint in the small pans and put a couple of sponge "brushes" in each color of paint.)

Distribute paper.

Say: **One way we can pray is to make pictures. Paint a picture about something you can talk to God about. While you're painting,**

think about what you'd like to say to God.

Show kids how to dab paint onto the paper. Tell kids that when they want to use a different color, they should use a brush that's already been in that color. As kids are painting, ask questions such as "What are you painting?" and "What would you say to God?" Praise the children for their work.

Say: **These are all great pictures. We can talk to God about all of these things. God wants us to talk to him about everything.**

5. Where Can I Pray?

Play this version of Duck, Duck, Goose to show kids they can pray anywhere.

Have kids stand in a circle. Say: **God wants us to talk to him any time, no matter where we are. Let's play a game to see where we can talk to God.**

Choose a volunteer to walk around the outside of the circle and lightly tap each child on the head, asking "Where?" each time. When the volunteer asks, "Where can I pray?" he or she and the tapped child must run around the circle in different directions. The first one to get back and yell out one place where kids can pray is safe. The other child must then go around and tap the children. It's okay if kids repeat the answers. But if kids keep saying the same thing or if they get stumped, you can whisper responses in their ears. Continue for several minutes.

Say: **Those are great ideas about where we can pray. God wants us to talk to him no matter where we are.**

6. A Thankful Prayer

(You'll need a favorite treat such as

cookies and milk. You'll also need napkins.)

Say: **One thing we can tell God is thank you. God has given us lots of wonderful gifts. Let's thank him now for this terrific snack.**

Offer a prayer of thanks. Serve the treats.

7. A Song About Prayer

Say: **God listens when we talk to him. Let's learn a song to help us remember to pray!**

Sing the following song to the tune of "London Bridge." Do the actions as you sing.

He is listening all the time, all the time, all the time!
He is listening all the time, when we talk to God!
(Cup hands to ears and point to a watch or clock)

Bow our heads, say, "Thank you Lord, thank you Lord, thank you Lord!"
Bow our heads, say, "Thank you Lord," when we talk to God!
(Bow heads)

Fold our hands and ask for help, ask for help, ask for help!
Fold our hands and ask for help, when we talk to God!
(Fold hands)

Close our eyes and praise his name, praise his name, praise his name!
Close our eyes and praise his name, when we talk to God!
(Close eyes)

When we're happy, shout for joy, shout for joy, shout for joy!

**When we're happy shout for joy,
when we talk to God!**
*(Cup hands to mouth and sing
loudly)*

**Listen to what God will say, God
will say, God will say!
Listen to what God will say,
when we talk to God!**
*(Cup hands over ears and sing
softly)*

**Watch and see what God will do,
God will do, God will do!
Watch and see what God will do,
when we talk to God!**
*(Cup hands around eyes like
binoculars)*

8. Let's Pray

(You'll need a playground ball.)

Have kids think of something they want to say to God. Then gather kids in a circle. Stand in the middle and gently bounce the ball to a child. When the child catches the ball, have him or her say the prayer to God and then bounce the ball back to you. Bounce the ball to children randomly until everyone has prayed.

by Patti Chromey

PUPPET PAGE

Photocopy and cut out enough puppets for each child to have one. Have children color them and attach Popsicle sticks to the backs to make puppets.

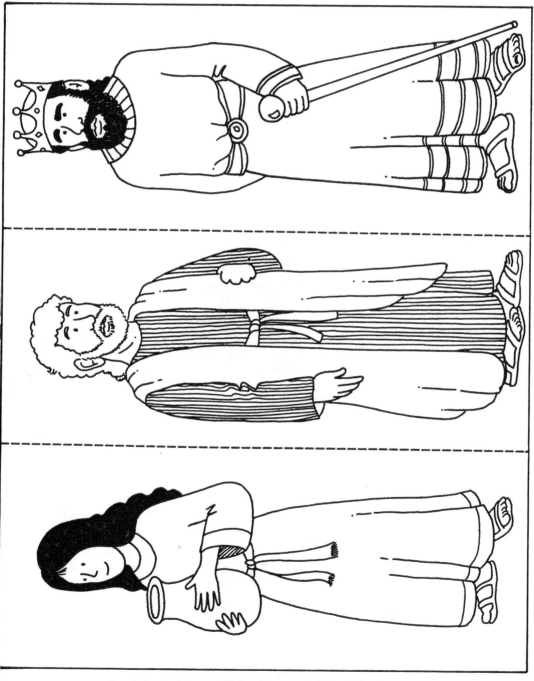

PUPPET PAGE

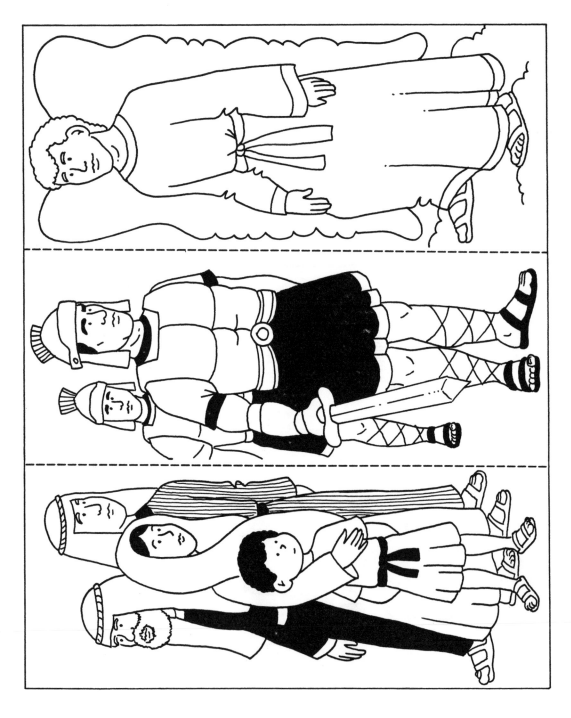

GOD CARES WHEN I'M SCARED

From the eyes of a child, the world can be a scary place. Beyond the common fears of barking dogs and the dark, children today express anxiety about the possibility of war, divorce and even death. There is little their eyes and ears don't catch from television or adult conversations.

Use this lesson to help kids feel God cares about their fears. God is always near to comfort us when we're afraid.

A POWERFUL PURPOSE

Children will discover God cares about their fears.

A LOOK AT THE LESSON

1. When Are You Afraid? (up to 5 minutes)
2. Tickle Monster (up to 5 minutes)
3. Elijah Was Scared (5 to 10 minutes)
4. God Is With Me (up to 5 minutes)
5. God Watches Me (up to 5 minutes)
6. What Can I Do? (5 to 10 minutes)
7. God's Eyes (up to 5 minutes)
8. Let's Thank God (up to 5 minutes)

A SPRINKLING OF SUPPLIES

Gather pictures from magazines of things children may be afraid of, a Bible, peanut butter, round crackers, banana slices, raisins, plastic knives and napkins.

THE LIVELY LESSON

1. When Are You Afraid?

(Before the children arrive, select several pictures from magazines of things children may be afraid of; for example, a big dog, bugs, a dark room or an angry-faced person.)

Gather the kids in an open area. As you show them each picture, ask:

● **Is this something that might scare you?**

● **Why does it seem scary?**

After looking at the pictures, ask the children to share other things they're afraid of. Some children may be embarrassed to share their fears. Empathize with the children and agree their fears are valid. Share things that scare you.

Say: **It sounds like all of us have times when we're scared. God cares about how we feel. Let's learn how God can help us when we're scared.**

2. Tickle Monster

Say: **God knows that sometimes we get scared. God made sure**

people would help us when we're afraid.

Play a game of Tickle Monster. You are the tickle monster who roams about the room tickling children. Ham it up with roars, chomping teeth and "scary" faces. But don't be so ferocious that you genuinely scare the children. Tell kids the only way to escape being tickled is to hold hands with another person. Anyone who dares to let go can be tickled until they grab a friend's hand.

Be sensitive to children who don't want to be touched or tickled.

Say: **When you are with someone else, things don't seem as scary. Even the tickle monster can't get you!**

Ask:

● **Who helps you feel better when you're afraid?**

3. Elijah Was Scared

(You'll need a Bible.)

Ask:

● **What do you do when you're afraid?**

Say: **Let's see what one man in the Bible did when he was afraid.**

Open the Bible to the story of Elijah in 1 Kings 19. Tell this story and have the children act it out.

Say: **A long time ago a wicked queen named Jezebel got mad at one of God's messengers, who was named Elijah. Jezebel said she was going to kill Elijah.**

That scared Elijah. He thought he was the only one left in the whole country who followed God. Elijah felt all alone. He thought there was no one who could help him. He was so scared by what Jezebel said that he ran away. (Have kids run in place) **He ran and ran and finally**

ended up in the desert.

When he got to the desert, he was tired from running. He curled up under a tree and fell asleep. (Have kids curl up and pretend to be asleep)

God knew that Elijah was scared, and God wanted to take care of Elijah. So after Elijah had slept for a while, an angel woke him up and gave him some food to eat and water to drink to strengthen him for a long journey. (Have kids pretend to eat and drink) **Elijah traveled on his long journey to a mountain called Mount Sinai and spent the night in a cave.**

God said to Elijah, "Why are you here?"

Elijah answered, "All the people have turned against you. I am the only one left, and they're trying to kill me, too."

Then God said, "Go stand outside and I will come by you."

Then a strong wind started to blow. (Have kids make wind sounds) **It made the rocks break into pieces. But God wasn't in the wind.**

Next, a powerful earthquake happened. (Have kids make earthquake sounds) **But God wasn't in the earthquake.**

Then there was a fire. (Have kids shield their faces from the fire) **But God wasn't in the fire, either.**

Then Elijah heard a very quiet, gentle sound. (Have kids make a quiet, gentle sound such as "Shhh") **Elijah knew this was God. So he went out to meet God.**

God told Elijah to go to a place where people still followed God. God knew Elijah wouldn't be as scared if other people were around to help him. Elijah wasn't scared

anymore, and he knew he wouldn't have to run away again because God would take care of him.

4. God Is With Me

Say: **The Bible says we don't have to be afraid because God is with us all the time.**

Move to the child closest to you. Put your arm around him or her and say: **(Name) and I are afraid of (let child say what he or she is afraid of). What does God say to us?** Have the kids say, "God is with you" and squeeze in to give the child a group hug. Repeat this with each child in the class.

Say: **Each time we're afraid, we can remember God is with us.**

5. God Watches Me

Have children act out this rhyme several times with you:

God is with me day and night.
When it is dark (cover eyes with hands),
When it is light (remove hands from eyes),
He is always watching me (cup hands around eyes like a pair of binoculars).
Wherever I am (turn around in a circle with arms stretched out),
He can see (touch eyes).
And God will take care of me (hug self).

6. What Can I Do?

Have kids form pairs by grabbing the hand of someone who's close to them. Have them sit down next to their partners.

Say: **Nobody likes to be afraid. Let's think of some things we can do when we're afraid or when our friends are afraid.**

Bring out the scary pictures from the When Are You Afraid? activity or use the fears kids mentioned in God Is With Me. Show kids one of the pictures or mention one of the fears and ask:

● **What could you do if you were afraid of this?**

After kids answer, have them act out what they would do.

Then ask:

● **What could you do if your partner were afraid of this?**

After they've answered, have them act out what they would do for their partners.

7. God's Eyes

(You'll need peanut butter, round crackers, banana slices, raisins, plastic knives and napkins.)

Have kids spread peanut butter onto round crackers. Cover with banana slices and top with raisins.

Say: **These crackers look like eyes. If you put two next to each other, you could pretend these eyes are God's eyes watching you to know when to help and protect you.**

Enjoy the snack.

8. Let's Thank God

Say: **Let's thank God for taking care of us when we're scared.**
Gather kids in a circle and pray, thanking God for his care and his protection.
by Mike and Amy Nappa

WHEN I'M LONELY

Kindergartners know what it's like to be lonely. Like people of all ages, they can be in a crowd of people and still feel like they're all alone. But kindergartners don't have the maturity older people have to deal with those feelings. Kindergartners may not even be able to identify their feelings. All they know is they feel bad. Some children react by whining, complaining and acting up. Others become silent and withdrawn.

Use this lesson to help kids recognize when they feel lonely and to give them positive skills to cope with those feelings.

A POWERFUL PURPOSE

Children will learn to recognize feelings of loneliness and will discover creative ways to cope with loneliness.

A LOOK AT THE LESSON

1. Freeze-the-Feeling Parade (5 to 10 minutes)
2. A Lonely Feeling (5 to 10 minutes)
3. The Lonely Only (5 to 10 minutes)
4. What to Do? (8 to 10 minutes)
5. Occupied (up to 5 minutes)
6. I Can (5 to 10 minutes)
7. Share a Snack (5 to 10 minutes)
8. Huggable Prayer (up to 5 minutes)

A SPRINKLING OF SUPPLIES

Gather dolls, stuffed animals, a Bible, a box of various items, cans with lids, construction paper, glue, scissors, markers, craft supplies, photocopies of the "I Can" handout, powdered milk, honey, peanut butter, bowls, spoons and wet washcloths.

THE LIVELY LESSON

1. Freeze-the-Feeling Parade

Tell children they're going to participate in a special parade. But before they do, they have to practice making the different faces they'll need to use in the parade.

Have kids line up in a row at the front of the room. Call out these feelings and encourage the children to really ham it up in displaying these feelings. Call out: **angry, sad, lonely, happy, excited, scared, tired, hungry.**

After they've practiced, have the kids march around the room. As they march, call out a feeling and have kids stop where they are and display the feeling. Then continue the parade. After you've called out all the emotions, stop the parade.

Say: **Today we're going to talk about one of these feelings that all of us have felt. We're going to talk about feeling lonely. Everybody feels lonely at times. We feel lonely when we don't have anyone to play with or talk to.**

2. A Lonely Feeling

(You'll need enough dolls and

stuffed animals for everyone to have one.)

Let each child pick out a doll or stuffed animal.

Say: **Let's find out what it feels like to be lonely. Pretend that all these toys got together to play.** Have kids put their toys all together in a group.

Say: **The toys were going to play dress-up and have a party. They were very excited because playing together was lots of fun. But, when this toy came to the party** (pick up one of the toys), **the other toys said they didn't want to play with it.** Move the toy away from the rest of the toys.

Say: **This toy had to play all by itself.**

Ask:

● **How did this toy feel?**

● **What do you think the toy did?**

Tell about a time you've felt lonely. Then have kids find partners by grabbing the hand of someone close by. Have partners tell each other about a time they felt lonely. Wander among the pairs to help them think of lonely times. Then form a circle.

Ask:

● **How does it feel to be lonely?**

3. The Lonely Only

(You'll need a Bible.)

Open the Bible to Matthew 26:36-45.

Say: **We aren't the only ones who feel lonely sometimes. Jesus felt lonely, too. Listen to this story about when Jesus felt very lonely.**

One night Jesus went with his friends to a garden. He said to them, "Peter, you and James and John stay here with me. The sadness in my heart tonight is so big and heavy that it's almost crushing me."

Jesus knew soon he would die and he wanted the three men to keep him company while he prayed. "Stay here," he said, "and stay awake with me."

Jesus fell to the ground and prayed hard. He cried to God to keep him alive. Then Jesus said to God, "But I will do whatever you want me to do."

Then Jesus got up and went over to Peter, James and John, but they had fallen asleep.

That made Jesus feel very lonely. He asked them, "How is it you three weren't able to stay awake with me even for an hour?"

Once more Jesus went away and prayed. Then he went back to Peter, James and John. Again he found them asleep. They couldn't keep their eyes open. Jesus asked them again to stay awake and pray with him.

Again Jesus left them to pray. When he came back, they were asleep again. Jesus said, "Are you still sleeping?"

Ask:

● **How do you think Jesus felt that night in the garden?**

● **How could his friends have helped?**

● **What can you do when you know that someone is lonely?**

Say: **Jesus needed his friends to be with him during this time, but they kept falling asleep. Jesus felt very lonely. When Jesus felt lonely, he turned to God and talked to God through prayer.**

4. What to Do?

Say: **It's no fun to feel lonely.**

Ask:

● **What kinds of things do you do**

when you feel lonely?

● **What do you say to your parents when you want someone to play with?**

Say: **Let's look at some good things to do when we feel lonely and some not-so-good things to do when we feel lonely.**

Ask:

● **How many of you know what it means to whine or complain?**

Say: **Let's use our best whiney voices to say, "I'm lonely!"** Lead kids in doing this. Then ask:

● **Is this a good thing to do when we're lonely?**

● **How does it feel to whine and complain?**

● **Does whining and complaining make the loneliness go away?**

Have kids practice the good and bad responses to loneliness listed below. After each one, ask them how it makes them feel and whether it makes the loneliness go away. Use these loneliness responses:

● **Ask calmly, "Mommy, would you play with me?"**

● **Throw a toy across the room, pout and say, "Nobody ever wants to play with me!"**

● **Pull out a toy to play with by yourself.**

● **Look at a book.**

● **Watch television.**

● **Draw on the wall.**

Say: **Some of these things are good to do when we're lonely and some aren't. Let's look at some more things we can do when we're feeling lonely.**

5. Occupied

(You'll need a box of various items such as a telephone, Legos, puzzles, a book, crayons and paper, a picture of

an ear and a dust cloth. Have enough items for each child to have one.)

Bring out the box of items. Give each child an item and ask children to think of things they could do with that item when they feel lonely. For example, kids could ask to call a friend on the telephone or use the trash can to clean their rooms. Encourage even the most outlandish ideas! The more creative children are, the better they'll be able to deal with loneliness.

6. I Can

(You'll need a can with a lid for each child, construction paper, glue, scissors, markers, craft supplies such as fabric scraps, tissue paper and yarn. You'll also need to photocopy and cut apart enough of the "I Can" slips for each child to have a few.)

Give each child a can with a lid, such as a coffee can, to decorate with construction paper, glue, markers and other craft supplies.

After their cans are decorated, say: **I have 10 things that we can do when we're lonely written on slips of paper. You can each put a few of these slips in your "I Can." Whenever you're lonely, you can choose something out of your "I Can" to do to help you stop being lonely.**

I'll read these slips one at a time. If you think this is a good thing that you'd like to do when you feel lonely, come to me, get a slip and put it in your can.

Read aloud each "I Can" slip. After all the slips are read, say: **Your "I Can" will remind you that you can do something when you're lonely.**

7. Share a Snack

(You'll need powdered milk, honey, peanut butter, bowls and spoons.

You'll also need wet washcloths for before and after cleanup.)

Form groups of three. Say: **We're going to share a snack today so we won't be lonely. God wants us to be good friends to each other so we won't be lonely at church.**

Have kids wash their hands. If you notice some kids have colds or unprotected scrapes, assign them tasks such as dumping the ingredients into the bowls so they won't touch the food. Give each of the following ingredients to a different group member: 1/3 cup powdered milk, 2/3 tablespoon honey, 2/3 cup peanut butter. Give each group a bowl and a spoon. Have kids mix their ingredients together in the bowl.

Have the kids divide the dough between them. You may need to help so portions are equal. Also, if kids have colds or unprotected scrapes, hand out the portions of dough instead of letting kids touch other kids' dough. Have kids use their dough to create faces that show how they feel about having good friends at church. Or let them use gingerbread-people cookie cutters to make "friends" out of the dough. Then let kids eat their dough.

8. Huggable Prayer

Have children hold hands in a circle. Say: **Let's talk to God and tell him how we feel when we're lonely, and let's ask him to help us when we're lonely.**

Let children pray. You can lead the prayer if none of the children want to pray. Then have kids squeeze together for a big group hug.

by Christine Yount

I CAN

Make several photocopies of this handout and cut apart the slips.

Look at a book.

Pray.

Put together a puzzle.

Pretend to be an astronaut.

Draw a picture.

Build a tent using a blanket and chairs.

Clean my room.

Play with a ball.

Call someone on the phone.

Help my parents with what they're doing.

WAY TO OBEY

Obedience is hard to learn. Of all God's creations, humans alone can choose their own way. We tend to overuse our freedom, forgetting the benefits of choosing to obey the God who made us. It's difficult to choose obedience over independence when in our limited sight, our own choices seem best.

Kindergartners aren't immune to the pull of rebellion. They are learning to aggressively put their own desires first. Use this lesson to teach them that the rewards of obedience are preferable to the potential hazards of independence.

A POWERFUL PURPOSE

Children will gain a better understanding of why it's important to obey God, parents and teachers.

A LOOK AT THE LESSON

1. To Paint a Fish (10 to 12 minutes)
2. Mother May I? (up to 5 minutes)
3. Traffic (up to 5 minutes)
4. A Whale of a Story (5 to 10 minutes)
5. Fish Food (up to 5 minutes)
6. A Promise Song (up to 5 minutes)
7. Thanks for Rules (up to 5 minutes)

A SPRINKLING OF SUPPLIES

Gather newspapers, a large appliance box, blue and black tempera paint, paintbrushes, paint shirts, masking tape, a whistle, four sheets or tablecloths, a Bible, finger Jell-O cut in fish shapes, juice, napkins and paper cups.

THE LIVELY LESSON

1. To Paint a Fish

(You'll need newspapers, a large appliance box with the panels on the ends cut off, blue and black tempera paint, paintbrushes and paint shirts.)

Ask two or three children to help lay newspapers on the floor. Have several children pull the appliance box onto the newspaper. Have the children use blue tempera paint to paint the outside of the box to look like a fish. Add eyes, scales and other features with black tempera paint. When the fish is completed, say: **This is a great fish! Thank you for obeying when I asked you to help. It made painting this fish much easier.**

2. Mother May I?

(You'll need masking tape.)

With masking tape, mark a starting line and a finish line on opposite sides of the room. Have kids stand at the starting line and wait until you tell them to move. Give clear instructions to individual kids. For example, tell Bobby to take two giant steps; tell Sarah to take three frog leaps; and tell Jonathon to take one baby step. Tell them that after the command of steps is given, they must ask, "Mother may I?" before they take any steps. If they don't ask permission, they must go back to the starting line. Don't go too fast or kids may get frustrated with this game. Remind them of the rules if they forget.

After kids have reached the finish line, ask:

● **How did you feel when you remembered to ask, "Mother may I?"**

● **How did you feel when you forgot to ask and had to go back to the starting line?**

Say: **Sometimes it's hard to remember all the rules we have to follow, just like it was hard to always remember to ask, "Mother may I?" Sometimes we don't want to follow the rules. Let's find out why it's important to obey.**

3. Traffic

(You'll need an attention-getting device such as a whistle and four sheets or tablecloths.)

Spread out four sheets or tablecloths with space in between them. The fabric will represent four "city blocks" and the aisles will be "roads." Fold the fabric to fit the size of your room, leaving plenty of aisle space for kids to walk in. Have children hold on to each other's waists bunny-hop style to form various kinds of vehicles. Two kids might form a sports car. Four kids could be a bus. One child could be a motorcycle or a pedestrian.

Tell the kids that when you blow the whistle, traffic will start to move. When you yell "Rush hour!" traffic must "flow" as quickly as it can. After a few minutes of rush-hour traffic, blow the whistle to stop traffic.

Have kids sit on the floor. Ask:

● **What kinds of traffic rules did you obey as we played traffic?**

● **What happened during rush hour when everyone drove so fast?**

● **What would happen if people drove real cars the way you drove the pretend cars?**

Say: **It's important to obey rules. People can get hurt if they don't follow the rules. Let's find out about a man in the Bible who didn't want to obey God.**

4. A Whale of a Story

(You'll need the painted fish box and a Bible.)

Show kids the book of Jonah in the Bible as you begin this story: **A long time ago, there lived a man named Jonah. One day God spoke to Jonah and said, "Jonah, I want you to travel to the city of Nineveh** (point to a corner of the room) **and tell them to stop doing bad things and start obeying me."**

But Jonah didn't want to go to Nineveh. So he got up and ran as fast as he could in the other direction (point to the opposite corner of the room). **Jonah thought that if he could run away fast enough, he could hide where God would never find him.**

Let's try to find the best hiding place in our room and hide from God. Have everyone run to find someplace in the room where God can't find them. As you go around the room, tag each child as you find him or her and say: **This was a good hiding place, but I still found you, and I know God could find you, too.** Have kids return to the gathering spot when you tag them.

When everyone is gathered again continue the story. Say: **Jonah ran and ran to hide from God. He didn't know yet, like we do, that you can't hide from God _anywhere_.**

Soon he came to the sea, but it wasn't far enough away, so Jonah got on a big boat to sail across the wide sea.

As soon as the boat set sail, the wind started to blow. All the sailors got scared because they were afraid the boat would sink. Jonah knew that God had found him, so he made the sailors throw him into the sea. At once, the sea became calm.

But, Jonah was swallowed by a big fish. Lead the kids over to the fish box and have them sit inside the box.

Say: **Jonah was inside the fish for three days and three nights. Then he prayed, "God, I will keep my promises to you." God heard Jonah's prayer and caused the fish to spit out Jonah.**

God said, "Jonah, I want you to go to Nineveh *(point to the Nineveh corner you pointed to earlier)* and tell them to stop doing bad things and start obeying me."

Say: **This time Jonah went straight to Nineveh and told the people about God. The people in Nineveh were sorry they had disappointed God, so they stopped doing evil things and started to obey God.**

5. Fish Food

(Follow the recipe for finger gelatin on the back of a box of Jell-O. Cut the Jell-O in fish shapes. You'll also need juice, napkins and paper cups.)

Serve the snacks. As children eat, talk about ways to obey. Ask:

● **What rules do we need to obey? Why?**

● **Who do we need to obey? Why?**

● **What happens when we don't obey?**

● **Why is it hard to obey?**

Have children throw away their napkins and cups to help clean up.

6. A Promise Song

Sing this song to the tune of "Twinkle, Twinkle, Little Star":

**I promise always to obey,
My parents and teachers
  every day.
They love me so they'll ask me to,
Do what's right and good
  and true.
I promise always to obey,
It's what God's Word tells
  me to do.**

7. Thanks for Rules

Close with a prayer, praising God for protecting us and thanking him for helping us with the rules he's given us to obey.

by Janel Kauffman

I'm Glad You're You

It's important that kindergartners know they're special in God's eyes. They can understand that God planned them to be special people, no matter what they look like or what they can or can't do.

Use this lesson to teach children that each of them has unique talents and is a wonderful creature made by a loving God.

A POWERFUL PURPOSE

Children will see how special they are in God's eyes.

A LOOK AT THE LESSON

1. This Is What I Like (5 to 10 minutes)
2. I'm the Only One of Me (8 to 10 minutes)
3. God Made Me Wonderful (up to 5 minutes)
4. A Special Sign (5 to 10 minutes)
5. Sarah and Abraham's Special Baby (5 minutes)
6. Gingerbread-Me Cookies (8 to 10 minutes)
7. A Special Prayer (up to 5 minutes)

A SPRINKLING OF SUPPLIES

Gather paper, a marker, tape, newspapers, yarn, scissors, tempera paint, bowls, a hand mirror, small paintbrushes, vegetable shortening, cornstarch, food coloring, a doll, a baby blanket, a Bible, iced gingerbread-people cookies, colored coconut, small candies, milk, paper cups and napkins.

THE LIVELY LESSON

1. This Is What I Like

(You'll need two sheets of paper, one with a happy face drawn on it and the other with a sad face drawn on it. Tape the two sheets of paper to opposite walls in your classroom.)

Show children the two faces you've taped to the walls. Tell the children that as you call out each item on the list below, they should run to the happy face if they like it or run to the sad face if they don't like it. Call these out one at a time: **birthday parties, lightning, snowball fights, peanut butter sandwiches, taking out the garbage, baseball, books, Barbie dolls, rainy days, hamsters, cleaning your room, red wagons.**

Gather children in an open area. Say: **Not everyone likes the same things.**

Ask:

● **Why doesn't everyone like the same things?**

Say: **God made each one of us special. None of us is exactly like anyone else. We all have different things we like and don't like.**

2. I'm the Only One of Me

(You'll need newspapers, paper, yarn, scissors and tempera paint in small bowls.)

Protect your work area with newspapers. Distribute paper. Have kids fold their sheets of paper in half and then open the paper like a book. Have them dip pieces of yarn in the paint and arrange the yarn on one side of the paper with one end of the yarn sticking out over the edge of the paper. Use more than one color of paint, but dip each piece of yarn in only one color.

Have kids fold the paper over the yarn and press so the paint touches both sides of the paper. Then have them pull the yarn out of the folded paper by the ends that are sticking out. When each sheet of paper is unfolded, you'll see a unique design.

YARN DESIGNS

Say: **Everyone used the same ingredients to make their paintings, but each one of them is different and special. Each of you is a person, but you're all different, too. God made each of you to be a special work of art.**

Put aside the paintings to dry.

3. God Made Me Wonderful

(You'll need a hand mirror.)

Say: **God made each of us special. The Bible says God made my whole self. I praise God because he made me in an amazing and wonderful way. What God has done is wonderful. Let's sing a song that talks about how special we are.**

Teach kids this song to the tune of "Twinkle, Twinkle, Little Star." Have children stand in a circle and pass around the hand mirror as you sing this song several times through. Have children look at themselves in the mirror as it comes to each of them.

God made me and God made you.
We're wonderful and special, too.
All of me he made to be,
Different from who's next to me.
God made me and God made you.
We're wonderful and special, too.

4. A Special Sign

(You'll need face paint, small paintbrushes and bowls. To make the face paint, mix together ½ cup vegetable shortening and ½ cup cornstarch in a bowl. When well blended, divide into small bowls and add food coloring. If you have more than 10 kids, or if you want more than two colors, make two batches of paint.)

Let children choose their favorite colors. Paint a symbol on each child's face that says he or she is special. Choose from symbols such as a star, a happy face, a heart, a flower, or the words "Wow!" or "Super!"

While you paint each child's face, tell them one reason they're special. For example, say: "Julie, I'm putting a happy face on your cheek. You're special because you always smile."

Tell kids not to touch the paint because it'll smear.

5. Sarah and Abraham's Special Baby

(You'll need a doll wrapped in a baby blanket and a Bible. Check the church nursery if you don't have a baby blanket.)

Gather kids in an open area. Pass

around the doll. Tell children to pretend it's a real baby and treat it gently. Open the Bible to Genesis 18:1-16.

Ask:

● **What do you like about babies?**

● **What don't you like about babies?**

● **What makes babies special?**

Say: **There's a story in the Bible about a couple who wanted a baby very much.**

Abraham and Sarah wanted a baby, but they thought they were too old. They were older than grandparents are.

But one day three men came to visit. Abraham and Sarah served good food for their visitors to eat. While the visitors were eating, God told Abraham that Sarah would have a baby. The baby was to be very special. God planned for Abraham and Sarah's baby to do important things.

When Sarah found out, she laughed and thought, "We're too old to have a baby."

But Sarah did have a baby. Abraham and Sarah loved the baby very much. Abraham and Sarah named the baby Isaac, which means laughter, because they were so happy that God had given them a baby.

At one time, each of you was a baby. Each of you was just as special as Isaac was when he was born. God has made each of you to do good things.

6. Gingerbread-Me Cookies

(You'll need baked and iced gingerbread-people cookies, colored coconut and small candies such as red hots, sprinkles, chocolate chips and raisins. You'll also need milk, paper cups and napkins.)

Have children use the coconut and candies to decorate the gingerbread people to look like themselves. After children finish decorating, pass out paper cups of milk and enjoy the snack. As they're eating "themselves," have each one of them tell how they're special.

7. A Special Prayer

Have children stand in a circle. Walk around the circle, giving each child a hug as you say his or her name in this prayer: **Thank you, God, for making us special. You made (Child's name) special and (Child's name) special...** Keep going until every child has been hugged and prayed for. Then pray: **Thank you, God, for all the important things you have for us to do. Amen.**

by Janel Kauffman

I'M A STAR

Paul writes in his letter to the Philippians that God's children shine like stars in a dark world. Kindergartners can "twinkle" as brightly as any other member of God's family.

Give your kids this opportunity to shine. They'll learn how God's light can shine through them to illuminate an entire world.

You can use this lesson as an alternative to Halloween or to celebrate All Saints' Day.

A POWERFUL PURPOSE

Kindergartners will learn that God's light will shine through their lives when they follow him.

A LOOK AT THE LESSON

1. Pumpkin Patch Art (up to 5 minutes)
2. Shining Examples (up to 5 minutes)
3. Turn On Your Light (5 to 10 minutes)
4. This Little Light of Mine (up to 5 minutes)
5. A Pumpkin Full of Goodness (up to 5 minutes)
6. Smile Makers (up to 5 minutes)
7. Stuff a Pumpkin (up to 5 minutes)
8. A Circle of Light (up to 5 minutes)

A SPRINKLING OF SUPPLIES

Gather yellow construction paper, scissors, tape, seasonal decorations, a flashlight, white paper lunch bags, orange crayons or orange tempera paint and paintbrushes, a Bible, a highlighting marker, a container with a lid, a pumpkin, a sharp knife, a small flashlight or a candle and matches, round cookies, orange frosting, plastic knives, raisins, candy corn, juice, paper cups, glue, newspaper and green ribbon.

Before class, set up each activity in a different area of the room. Cut out enough pairs of footprints from yellow construction paper to create a winding path that leads to each activity area. Decorate the room with seasonal decorations such as orange and yellow balloons and crepe paper streamers. Arrange to have access to a room or closet with no windows or with covered windows so it can be made very dark.

THE LIVELY LESSON

1. Pumpkin Patch Art

(You'll need a flashlight, one white paper lunch bag per child, and orange crayons or orange tempera paint and paintbrushes.)

As children enter the room, welcome them and tell them to follow you to the first activity. Shine a flashlight on the yellow footprints as you lead them.

Give each child a white paper bag to color or paint.

Say: **We're going to make special pumpkins with these bags.**

After everyone has colored or painted their bags orange, say: **We'll finish our pumpkins later. Follow me to the next activity.**

If you use paint, set the bags aside to dry.

2. Shining Examples

(You'll need a highlighting marker and a flashlight. Highlight Isaiah 2:5 in either a King James Version or New International Version of the Bible.)

Say: **The yellow footprints we followed to this area remind me of a verse in the Bible.**

Show the highlighted words of Isaiah 2:5 in the Bible. Read the verse. Then teach the following song to the tune of "The Mulberry Bush":

**Come, let us walk in
The light of the Lord,
The light of the Lord,
The light of the Lord.
Come, let us walk in
The light of the Lord,
'Cause the Bible tells us so.**

Sing this song several times as you lead the kids around the room shining the flashlight on the path of footprints.

Ask:

● **When you walk into a dark room, what's the first thing you do? Why?**

Say: **The Bible says God is light. When we walk in God's light, we do things that please him.**

Ask:

● **What kinds of things can we do that will please God?**

As you move to the next area, sing the Bible verse again as you follow the footprints.

3. Turn On Your Light

(You'll need a Bible, a flashlight and a container with a lid that won't let the flashlight's light shine through.)

Take children into a room that can be made very dark. Leave the lights on until everyone is inside the room. Have everyone sit very close together and hold hands so that when the lights are turned off, they'll know someone is close by.

Turn off the lights. Kids may be anxious in the dark so be sure you don't prolong the amount of time the lights are off.

Say: **It sure is dark in here. We came in here for our Bible verse, but it's too dark to read. It's a good thing I brought a flashlight.**

Bring out your flashlight and turn it on. Say: **That's much better. It's much easier to see everyone with the flashlight on. And now I can read this Bible verse. But, I'm afraid my flashlight will fall and break. Then we wouldn't have any light at all. I think I'll put it in this container so it will be safe. Then we can read the Bible verse.**

Put the flashlight in the container and shut the lid. Say: **Now all the light is gone again. I wonder what I should do.** Kids will probably giggle and tell you to take the flashlight out of the container.

Say: **That's a great idea. I need someone to hold it for me so it doesn't break.**

Ask:

● **Where should you stand so we get the most light?**

Have kids experiment to find out how to get the best light by holding the light close to the floor, close to the Bible or pointed directly at someone from a close distance. Show them that when the light is held high, more people benefit from the light.

Say: **Now I can read the Bible**

verse. Read Matthew 5:14-16 from an easy-to-understand version of the Bible or use your own words.

Ask:

● **When can you see the light the best?**

● **What would this little room look like if everyone here was a flashlight?**

Say: **God wants us all to shine with the kind and loving things we do.**

Ask:

● **What are some kind and loving things we could do for God and for people we know?**

Say: **Those are great ideas! You'll fill up the whole world with God's light if you do all of those kind and loving things.**

4. This Little Light of Mine

(You'll need a flashlight.)

Sing the song "This Little Light of Mine" with the kids. Use the traditional words and motions, except change the word "bushel" to "basket."

Have kids sing this song as you lead them to the next activity with the flashlight shining on the footprints.

5. A Pumpkin Full of Goodness

(You'll need a pumpkin, a sharp knife, a small flashlight or a candle and matches. You'll also need a flashlight. Before class, carve a jack-o'-lantern. Save the pieces you cut from the pumpkin. Make sure your pumpkin has a happy face, not a sad or scary face. Light the pumpkin with a candle or small flashlight.)

Gather children in an open area of the room. Put the jack-o'-lantern in front of the kids so they can see the light. Turn out the lights in the room.

It's okay if some light comes in from the windows.

Say: **This pumpkin reminds me of how we look when we do loving things. God wants people to think of him when they see the loving things we do. Sometimes we forget to be loving. Sometimes we don't want to be loving.**

Ask:

● **What do you think happens when we do something that's unkind?**

Say: **Let me show you what happens. Name some things that are unkind or unloving.**

As a child names something, put one cutout piece of the pumpkin's face back in its place. Do this with each one until the light in the pumpkin can no longer be seen.

Ask:

● **What happened to the light?**

● **What covered up the light?**

Say: **Now let's name some loving things we can do to make the light of God shine from inside us.**

Remove a cutout piece each time a child mentions a loving deed. When the pieces are all removed, ask:

● **Which pumpkin do you like best?**

Sing "This Little Light of Mine" as you lead the kids to the next activity with the flashlight shining on the footprints.

6. Smile Makers

(You'll need a round cookie for each child, orange frosting, plastic knives, raisins, candy corn, juice, paper cups and a flashlight.)

Help children spread orange frosting on their cookies. Then have kids use raisins and candy corn to make happy faces on the cookies.

Say: **These "pumpkin" cookies have smiling faces. These smiles are like the ones our family and friends have on their faces when they see us do something loving. They smile because we are walking in the light of the Lord. Let's thank God for his light that shows us how to be loving.**

Offer a prayer. Serve juice.

When you are ready to lead the children to the next activity, sing the Bible verse from the Shining Examples activity as you shine the flashlight on the footprints.

7. Stuff a Pumpkin

(You'll need yellow construction paper, scissors, the orange-colored lunch bags, glue, newspaper, a 12-inch piece of green ribbon for each child and a flashlight.)

Have kids cut out construction paper noses, eyes and mouths to make faces for their paper-bag pumpkins.

As the children glue on the pieces, ask:

● **What can you do that will let God's light shine?**

Help children stuff wadded pieces of newspaper in their bags. Leave enough room at the top of each to close it by twisting the bag and tying it with green ribbon.

Lead kids to an open area with the light from the flashlight. Form a circle and have children hold hands.

8. A Circle of Light

(You'll need the paper-bag pumpkins and the jack-o'-lantern.)

Place the paper-bag pumpkins and the jack-o'-lantern in the middle of the circle of kids.

Say: **God's light shines in us when we do loving deeds for all the people around us.**

Pray: **God, thank you for making us shine with your light when we love other people.**

by Kathy Downs

PART 3:
A LIVELY LOOK
AT MY
RELATIONSHIPS

WORKING TOGETHER

C ooperation is essential for any group activity to be successful. Although kindergartners are starting to enjoy group activities, they lack the refined social skills it takes to work together well.

The activities in this lesson help children understand that working together can be fun, and it make things easier.

A POWERFUL PURPOSE

Kindergartners will learn that God created us to cooperate.

A LOOK AT THE LESSON

1. Building Together (up to 5 minutes)
2. Jerusalem's Wall (5 to 10 minutes)
3. Cleaning Together (up to 5 minutes)
4. Making a Snack Together (up to 5 minutes)
5. Our Body Works Together (up to 5 minutes)
6. People Work Together (5 to 10 minutes)
7. Making Music Together (up to 5 minutes)
8. Wiggle Prayer (up to 5 minutes)

A SPRINKLING OF SUPPLIES

Gather building blocks, a Bible, modeling clay, a plastic trash bag, presweetened punch mix, a plastic pitcher of water, paper cups, a spoon and crackers.

THE LIVELY LESSON

1. Building Together

(You'll need building blocks such as wooden blocks or Lego building blocks. There should be enough blocks for each child to have several.)

Have children sit in a circle on the floor and give each child one block or Lego. Put the rest of the blocks away so kids don't have access to them.

Say: **We're going to have a race to see who can build the tallest building. Ready? Go!**

Kids will be perplexed because they only have one block each.

After a few seconds, look around for a tall tower. Say: **That race didn't work very well. Why?**

Say: **That's right. We need more than one block to build something.**

Ask:

● **What would happen if we put our blocks together?**

Give kids a chance to build something with their blocks. Get the rest of the blocks out. After they use a block, let them get another one to add to the building until they feel their work is complete. Compliment their work and creativity.

2. Jerusalem's Wall

(You'll need a Bible, modeling clay and a plastic trash bag.)

Gather the children in a circle. Say: **Watching you build with blocks made me think of a man in the**

Bible named Nehemiah. Nehemiah was a man who lived before Jesus was born. Here in the Old Testament is the book that Nehemiah wrote.

Open the Bible to the book of Nehemiah and show the kids where the book begins.

Pass out hunks of modeling clay to each child. Have children use their clay to make building stones while you tell the Bible story. Spread out the plastic trash bag in the middle of the circle and have kids put their stones on it.

Say: **There was a terrible war and the city of Jerusalem was destroyed. God's people were forced to march to another country to live. They lived there for many, many years, until God finally sent them back to Jerusalem.**

When they got back to Jerusalem, Nehemiah was worried because his people, the Jews, didn't have a safe place to live. Their enemies had torn down the wall around Jerusalem. The people of Jerusalem needed a wall around their city to protect them from people who wanted to hurt them.

Nehemiah couldn't build a wall by himself, just like you couldn't build a building with just one block. So he got a lot of his people together and they all worked together to build a huge wall. They hauled heavy beams into place and put in bolts and bars for locking the gates.

They had to work quickly because as long as there wasn't a wall around Jerusalem the people weren't protected.

While the Jews were building the wall, Nehemiah found out their enemies were planning to cause trouble. **So Nehemiah developed a plan. He told some people to build the wall. He told other people to carry materials to the wall. And he told some people to watch for enemies who would start a fight. Everyone had a different job, but they all worked together to build the wall as quickly as possible. Let's work together to make our own wall around Jerusalem.**

Have kids each contribute their stones to the clay wall. Say: **(Child's name), lay a stone to begin our wall. (Child's name), add a stone to the wall.** Continue until all the children have contributed their stones and you have a round wall.

Continue the story: **It took God's people a long time to build the wall around Jerusalem. Everyone had to help, just like everyone here helped build our wall. The work was very hard because they made the walls out of heavy stones that would protect the city. Because they all worked together, they got the wall built. Then they thanked God and had a big party with a lot to eat!**

JERUSALEM'S WALL

3. Cleaning Together

Say: **Why don't we have something to eat, too. But first we need to clean up. If I ask only one per-**

son to pick up the blocks, it will take a long time to get the room clean. Let's see how quickly it's cleaned if we all work together!

Race with the children to see how fast the blocks can all be returned to their container.

Then say: **If I ask only one person to put away the modeling clay, it will take a long time. Let's work together to put it away quickly.**

Work with the children to put the clay away quickly.

Say: **That was great! Working together sure makes things easier!**

4. Making a Snack Together

(You'll need crackers, presweetened punch mix, a plastic pitcher of water, a stack of paper cups and a large spoon.)

Say: **I brought some crackers for us, but I didn't have time to make a drink.**

Give several children one of the following items: presweetened punch mix, a plastic pitcher of water, a stack of paper cups and a spoon. You may want the kids to make two pitchers of punch so more kids can participate.

Say: **It would be nice to have some punch with our crackers.**

Ask:

● **Does anyone have any punch? What do you have? If we put all these things together, what would we have?**

Say: **Let's work together to make ourselves something to drink!**

Help each child use what they have. Let the children do the adding, mixing and pouring as much as possible. This is their chance to work together, even if it is a little messy.

5. Our Body Works Together

(You'll need crackers and the

punch.)

Put the crackers, along with the punch, on the table so the children can see them, but have kids sit on the other side of the room.

Say: **The different parts of our bodies work together every day. Let's see how. We are going to have our snack now, but the food is on the other side of the room.**

Ask:

● **What would happen if only our eyes worked? Would we be able to eat our snack?**

● **What would happen if only our feet worked? Would we be able to eat our snack?**

● **What would happen if only our hands worked? Would we be able to eat our snack?**

Say: **Let's have all of our body parts work together to get our snack into our stomachs!** Have kids walk across the room to get their snacks.

As children eat their snacks, ask them to name a few of their body parts that are working together to help them eat. Be sure to compliment them on the delicious drink.

6. People Work Together

Say: **Just like the parts of our body work together, we all need to work together to get things done.**

Ask:

● **What are some things your mom or dad does to help get things done at your home?**

● **What are things you do?**

Say: **Let's do some of those things now.**

Have kids each choose one of the things they do or their moms and dads do and act it out. Have the whole class act out their tasks at the same time.

After a few minutes call everyone back together.

Say: **In our church there are a lot of things that people do. What are some of them? Let's act those out, too.**

Have each child choose one of the things that people in the church do. Have everyone act out his or her task together. In a couple of minutes, call everyone back together.

Say: **At home and at church, people work together to make getting work done easier.**

7. Making Music Together

Say: **Another thing we can do together is make music.**

Sing the following song to the tune of "Mary Had a Little Lamb." Each time you say the word "you" point to a different child.

We work together, you (point to a child) **and me** (point to self),
You and me, you and me.
We work together, you and me,
To show our love for God.

We play together, you and me,
You and me, you and me.
We play together, you and me,
To show our love for God.

We sing together, you and me,

You and me, you and me.
We sing together, you and me,
To show our love for God.

Say: **We worked together today and got lots of different things done. Thank you all for sharing in the work and fun!**

8. Wiggle Prayer

Have kids act out this prayer while you read it: **Thank you, God, for making my body work together. My toes wiggle** (pause) **and my knees bend** (pause) **to help me walk** (pause). **It'd be much harder to walk if my toes didn't wiggle and my knees didn't bend** (pause).

My hands can pick up a glass (pause) **and my elbows bend** (pause) **to help me take a drink** (pause). **I might not be able to drink if I couldn't pick up things with my hands and bend my elbows** (pause).

Thank you, God, for giving me friends I can work together with. We can shake hands with each other (pause). **We can smile at each other** (pause). **And we can hold hands and make one big circle** (pause). **Getting our work done is so much friendlier when we help each other. Thank you, God, for making us able to help each other.**
                    by Mike and Amy Nappa

SAYING "I'M SORRY"

Sometimes the things we do hurt other people.

In a world where it's easier to look out for our own interests than to be loving to others, hurting people is unavoidable. It's important that we say "I'm sorry" when we hurt someone. But it's not easy to admit fault.

Kindergartners struggle with apologies just as adults do. Use this lesson to teach kindergartners how apologies can mend relationships.

A POWERFUL PURPOSE

Kindergartners will discover the importance of saying they're sorry when they're wrong.

A LOOK AT THE LESSON

1. Sometimes We Hurt Others (10 to 12 minutes)
2. Play-Doh Mistakes (up to 5 minutes)
3. Saying "I'm Sorry" Feels Good (5 to 10 minutes)
4. A Son Is Sorry (up to 5 minutes)
5. Let's Celebrate! (up to 5 minutes)
6. Saying "I'm Sorry" Is Hard (up to 5 minutes)
7. Let's Pray (up to 5 minutes)

A SPRINKLING OF SUPPLIES

Gather blocks, items for a home center, paper, scissors, glue, crayons, markers, Play-Doh, photocopies of the "Sorry Situations" handout, cupcakes, juice, paper cups and napkins.

THE LIVELY LESSON

1. Sometimes We Hurt Others

(You'll need activity areas with limited supplies such as a building block area with a few blocks, a home center with a few dishes and an art center with a few sheets of paper, one pair of blunt-end scissors, one bottle of glue, a few crayons and a few markers.)

As children arrive, let them choose which activity area they'd like to go to. Give them several minutes of playtime. Watch for problems such as children who aren't included, children who won't share or children who don't agree on what to do with the supplies. Don't step in to solve the problems.

After a few minutes, gather children together and ask:

● **What's fun about playing together?**

● **What makes it hard to play together?**

Point out specific conflicts and ask questions such as "Paul, how did you feel when Jonathon knocked over your block tower?" or "Samantha, how did you feel when Josie wouldn't share the scissors with you?"

Say: **Sometimes other people hurt us. And sometimes we hurt other people. It's important to say "I'm sorry" when we hurt people.**

Give kids an opportunity to say "I'm sorry" for any conflicts that occurred during the playtime.

2. Play-Doh Mistakes

(You'll need Play-Doh.)

Give yourself and each child a lump of Play-Doh and let everyone create objects. Admire the work of the children and show them what you made.

Ask:

● **Have you ever been looking at something that belongs to someone else and you accidentally break it?**

Break your own object in half.

Ask:

● **How do you feel when you accidentally break something?**

Say: **When we do something wrong we feel bad, especially if we do it by accident. But when we say we're sorry, it helps make things better.**

Repair your Play-Doh creation.

3. Saying "I'm Sorry" Feels Good

(You'll need the situations and emotion faces cut out from the "Sorry Situations" handout.)

Have children sit in a circle. Show them one of the situations and all of the emotion faces.

Ask:

● **What happened in this picture?**

● **How do the people in this picture feel?**

Have kids pick different faces to put in the picture. As the children put faces with each person to show how they feel, ask:

● **Why does this person feel (angry, sad, happy, sorry)?**

Point to each of the people in the picture and ask:

● **What would you do if you were this person?**

● **How would everyone in the** picture feel if this person (*point to the person in the picture who was mean or who hurt someone*) **said "I'm sorry"?** Have kids pick out faces to put in the picture.

Show kids the other situations and repeat the questions.

Say: **When we hurt someone, saying I'm sorry can help everybody feel better if we really mean it.**

4. A Son Is Sorry

Ask:

● **When has someone said "I'm sorry" to you?**

Tell a story about when someone said "I'm sorry" to you and how you felt.

Then say: **Jesus told a story once about a boy who hurt his father. When the boy grew into a young man, he wanted to leave home. He said, "Dad, give me some money," and then he moved far away. This made the father sad.**

The young man spent all the money that his father had given him on things he didn't really need. When all his money was gone, he got a job feeding pigs. He was so poor that he had to eat the pig food!

He knew he had done the wrong thing and decided to go back and say "I'm sorry" to his father. He started walking back home. When his father saw his son coming, he ran out to meet him.

The son said "I'm sorry." His father was so happy to see his son again that he forgave him. He said: "That's okay, Son. I'm glad you came home."

And they had a big party to celebrate the son coming home.

5. Let's Celebrate!

(You'll need cupcakes, juice, paper cups and napkins.)

Say: **Since the people in our Bible story had a party, let's have a party, too, to celebrate what we've learned today.**

Pass out cupcakes and juice. While you enjoy the snack, ask questions such as "What makes it hard to say 'I'm sorry'?" and "How do you feel when you say 'I'm sorry'?"

6. Saying "I'm Sorry" Is Hard

Say: **Sometimes saying you're sorry is hard to do. But we can do things even if they're hard. Hopping on one foot is hard to do, but I'll bet you can do it.** *(Have everyone hop on one foot)*

Turning a somersault is hard for some people, but it's easy if you practice. *(Have the children do somersaults)*

Skipping is hard to do. Have any of you learned to skip yet? *(Have the children skip)*

Say: **Lots of things seem hard to do, but when we practice, we can do them! Saying you're sorry is hard, but you've shown that you can do hard things.**

7. Let's Pray

Pray this prayer, pausing to let kids do the actions: **Thank you, God, for helping us do hard things. We can hop on one foot** *(pause)*. **We can turn somersaults** *(pause)*. **We can skip** *(pause)*. **And we can say "I'm sorry"** *(pause)*. **Help us to say "I'm sorry"** *(pause)* **when we need to. Amen.**

by Mike and Amy Nappa

SORRY SITUATIONS

Photocopy these two pages and cut out the situations and the emotion faces.

SORRY SITUATIONS

SHARING IS FUN

Children are constantly reminded to share. But it's hard to let someone else ride *your* bike, read *your* book or eat some of *your* cookies. Kids are naturally selfish; they're made that way. To them it's not fair to have to give away something that belongs to them. But by introducing them to the idea of sharing what they have with others, we can help develop in them a heart for generosity.

Use this lesson to help kindergartners learn that sharing can be fun.

A POWERFUL PURPOSE

Kindergartners will learn that sharing can be fun.

A LOOK AT THE LESSON

1. This Is Mine! (up to 5 minutes)
2. Sharing Feels Good! (up to 5 minutes)
3. A Boy Shares With Jesus (5 to 10 minutes)
4. Loaves and Fishes (up to 5 minutes)
5. I Can Share (up to 5 minutes)
6. We Share the World (up to 5 minutes)
7. Share a Hug (up to 5 minutes)
8. Pray to Share (up to 5 minutes)

A SPRINKLING OF SUPPLIES

Gather yarn or lightweight rope, a large balloon or beach ball, paper plates, a marker, biscuits, tuna salad, a bowl, a spoon, a basket, napkins, a drink, paper cups, paper and crayons.

THE LIVELY LESSON

1. This Is Mine!

(You'll need a 6-foot piece of yarn or lightweight rope and a large inflated balloon or beach ball.)

Tie the yarn between two chairs or doorknobs. Be sure the yarn is at least an inch or two above the head of the tallest child to avoid tangles. Bring out a balloon or beach ball.

Say: **Look at this ball that I brought. I want to play with it all by myself.** *(Dribble the ball and walk around the class)* **Sometimes I like to play ball alone. But I also like to share with my friends. Would anyone like to share this ball with me? Let's see how fun it can be to share this ball in a game.**

Divide the class in half and have children stand on either side of the yarn. Have them bat the ball or balloon back and forth over it. Encourage them to take turns. If any of the children seem to be "ball hogs," suggest that everyone sit down on their bottoms (not knees) and hit from this position. This will help them give others a turn. Do not keep score, count the number of hits or make much effort to keep the ball off the ground. Just play together and have fun.

After playing for a few minutes, gather the children into a circle.

2. Sharing Feels Good!

(You'll need two paper plates and a marker. Make one of the plates into a happy face. Make the other a sad face.)

Show kids the happy face and the sad face.

Ask:

● **Has anyone ever taken away a toy you were playing with and said: "That's mine. You can't play with it"?** Invite children to tell about their experiences.

● **How did that make you feel?** Have kids point to a paper-plate face and describe how they felt.

● **How do you feel when someone shares their things with you?** Have kids point to a paper-plate face and describe how they would feel.

● **What are some things you like to share with others?**

● **How do you feel when you share something?** Have kids point to a paper-plate face and describe how they would feel.

Say: **Sharing sure does make us feel good! It's fun to share!**

3. A Boy Shares With Jesus

(You'll need five small biscuits such as refrigerator biscuits, a small amount of tuna salad in a bowl, a spoon, a basket and napkins. If you have five or fewer in your class, make the biscuits smaller before you bake them. Watch them carefully while they bake! Smaller biscuits will take less time to bake than the package says.)

Say: **Once, a long time ago, a lot of people went to see Jesus and hear him teach. Hundreds and hundreds of people were there. There were more people than could fit into this whole building!**

They listened to Jesus all day. The people hadn't brought any food with them and they got very hungry. It was hard for them to listen to Jesus because they were so hungry. It got late and Jesus' friends began to worry. They didn't have any food for all the people. It would have taken a lot of money to buy enough food to feed everybody, and they didn't have much money.

In the crowd they found a boy who had brought five small loaves of bread and two small fish for his lunch. (*Bring out the biscuits and tuna that you've put in a basket*) **It wasn't a very big lunch; it was just enough for the boy. But the boy wanted to share his lunch with everyone else, so he gave his lunch to Jesus' friends.**

The loaves weren't big like the kind we buy at the store. They were probably about as big as one of these biscuits. Let's divide this food and have our snack.

Have one or two children distribute napkins and the biscuits. When they run out of biscuits, let them puzzle for a moment about how to feed everyone. Then, if they need help, suggest they tear the biscuits into pieces so that everyone gets a small piece. Then go around and put a small bite of tuna on each biscuit. Offer a prayer of thanksgiving, then enjoy the snack. After kids are finished, ask:

● **Did that snack fill you up or are you still hungry?**

Say: **Jesus' friends knew they'd need more food than this to fill up all the people. They didn't know what they were going to do to feed all the people, but they took the bread and the fish to Jesus.**

It wasn't much food, but Jesus

told everyone to sit down. Then he prayed for the food and began breaking off pieces and handing them out. All the people were surprised because there was enough food for everybody. All the people ate until they were full. There was even enough left to fill 12 baskets! This was one of the many miracles—the amazing things—that Jesus did.

4. Loaves and Fishes

(You'll need enough biscuits and tuna salad for everyone. You'll also need a drink and paper cups.)

Say: **We couldn't make a tiny bit of food fill up everybody in the class like Jesus did, so I brought extra food so each person will have enough. But let's thank God for it first.**

Bring out more biscuits and tuna salad. Serve the drinks. Pray a short prayer thanking God for providing food.

As the kids enjoy their snacks, ask questions such as "How did the boy feel when he gave his lunch to Jesus' friends?" and "How did Jesus feel when the boy shared his lunch?" Also ask them to tell about a time when they shared with others.

5. I Can Share

(You'll need paper and crayons.)
Ask:

● **If you could share a wonderful gift with someone who needs it, what would your gift be?**

● **Who would you give your gift to?**

Distribute a sheet of paper to each child. Put out enough crayons for everyone to have one. Kids will be able to color, but if they want to change colors they'll need to share with someone else. Have children draw pictures of the gift they'd give.

Watch the children closely. Disputes may arise over who gets what color. Don't intervene too quickly; give the kids an opportunity to work it out. If they can't resolve the conflict, gently remind them that sharing helps everyone. You may choose to hand out another crayon of that color. Or you may want to let one child use the crayon for a couple of minutes and then let the other child use the crayon for a couple of minutes.

Don't force the children to share and don't scold them for not sharing. At this age, kids are still very self-centered. While we can teach them about sharing, not all children will understand it enough to practice it willingly.

However, do praise the children when you see them sharing. Your positive comments will reinforce the lesson.

6. We Share the World

Say: **Sometimes it's hard to share our toys or our special things. But I know some things that are easy to share.**

Have everyone stand and join you in doing the following motions. Ask each question and wait for children's responses. There is one suggested answer for each question, but if you can think of a way to act out any of the children's answers, be sure to include those. Say:

It's easy to share the sunshine. (*Lift hands over head with fingers spread out*) **What's fun to do when we're sharing the sunshine? We can run.** (*Run around the room*)

It's easy to share the rain. (*Wiggle fingers while moving hands down*) **What's fun to do when we're sharing the rain? We can splash in puddles.** (*Stamp feet and pretend you're getting wet*)

It's easy to share the wind. (*Blow air*) **What's fun to do when we're sharing the wind? We can all fly our kites in the wind!** (*Hold an imaginary kite string. Pretend the kite is blowing higher and higher. Don't let anyone lose his or hers, and don't get it tangled in a tree!*)

It's easy to share a tree. (*Spread out arms as branches*) **What's fun to do with a tree? We can climb a tree.** (*Make climbing motions*) **And we can also rest in its shade.** (*Have everyone sit down*)

Say: **We really do have fun sharing all the things God has given us.**

7. Share a Hug

Say: **Another thing that's fun to share is love. Let's give each other one great big hug.**

Have children stand in a circle and put their arms around those standing at their sides. Count to three, and on "three" have everyone take a step toward the center and gently squeeze their friends.

8. Pray to Share

Say: **Today we shared a lot of different things. And it was fun! Let's ask Jesus to help us remember to share with each other.**

Close with a simple prayer, thanking God for sharing good things with us such as food, sunshine and rain. Ask God to help everyone remember that sharing is fun.

by Mike and Amy Nappa

GOD'S FAMILY AROUND THE WORLD

As kindergartners explore the world, they discover that people don't all look or act the same. They wear different clothes and eat unfamiliar foods. It's easy to make judgments based on our differences and make our circle of love exclusive. But God calls us to celebrate the qualities that make each person unique and make our circle big enough for everyone to feel at home.

Kindergartners need to understand that differences are good and that God planned for us to be different. Use this lesson to help children learn to accept others and realize God loves all people.

A POWERFUL PURPOSE

Children will discover ways that people are different and see that God loves people just the way they are.

A LOOK AT THE LESSON

1. Same and Different (up to 5 minutes)
2. God Made Everyone (up to 5 minutes)
3. Chopsticks (5 to 10 minutes)
4. A Different Bible Story (5 to 10 minutes)
5. Jesus Loves the Little Children (up to 5 minutes)

6. Pudding Paint (5 to 10 minutes)
7. A Fruity Snack (5 to 10 minutes)
8. Thanks for Differences (up to 5 minutes)

A SPRINKLING OF SUPPLIES

Gather Play-Doh, chopsticks or unsharpened pencils, a Bible, paper, small bowls, prepared vanilla pudding, food coloring, wet washcloths, exotic fruit, paper cups, a pitcher of cold water and napkins.

THE LIVELY LESSON

1. Same and Different

Say: **We're all alike in some ways and different in some ways. Let's find some ways we're alike.**

As you ask which characteristics kids share, have them form groups with the other kids who have that same characteristic. Don't pick characteristics that'll exclude one child. No one should feel left out. For example, if every child in your class has blond hair except for one child, don't group kids according to hair color. Choose a different characteristic such as liking the same cartoon show.

Ask:

● **Who has the same color hair?**

Say: **Everyone who has the same color hair stand together. Some of you are the same. Some are different.**

Ask:

● **Who has the same color eyes?**

Say: **Stand together if your eyes are the same.**

Ask:

● **Who has shoes like yours?**

● **Who has the same color shirt or dress as you?**

● **Who has the same name as you?**

Say: **There are some things about us that are different and some things that are the same. If we were all exactly the same, there'd be no way to tell us apart.**

2. God Made Everyone

(You'll need Play-Doh.)

Give children lumps of Play-Doh and ask them to shape an animal, real or imaginary. Encourage them in their creativity and comment on how unique each creation is.

Say: **Each one of you has made a different creature.** (Even if two children made dogs, they'll both look different.) **None of these creatures are exactly the same, but they're all special because they were made by you! We're all different from each other in some ways, but God loves us all because he created us! Let's learn about other ways people are different.**

3. Chopsticks

(You'll need Play-Doh. You'll also need a pair of chopsticks for each child. If you're unable to find chopsticks, substitute unsharpened pencils, but be sure to explain the substitution to the children.)

Have children use their Play-Doh to form balls about the size of Ping-Pong balls. Distribute chopsticks or unsharpened pencils.

Say: **Some people don't use forks and spoons. They use chopsticks instead. They hold both sticks in one hand and pick up pieces of meat, vegetables and balls of rice.**

Let's pretend these balls of Play-Doh are balls of rice. Can anyone pick up the rice ball? Give kids time to experiment.

Ask:

● **Would you like to eat with chopsticks all the time?**

Say: **People around the world eat their food in a lot of different ways. In some places, the people eat with their fingers.** Have kids pretend to eat their rice balls with their fingers.

Ask:

● **What would it be like to eat with your fingers all the time?**

Say: **In other parts of the world, people use big leaves instead of plates.**

Ask:

● **What would it be like to eat off of leaves instead of plates?**

Say: **People do things a lot of different ways. God made us all different.**

4. A Different Bible Story

(You'll need a Bible.)

Open the Bible to John 4.

Ask:

● **How is everyone the same?** Children may give responses such as everyone eats, everyone breathes or God made everyone.

Say: **We're all the same in two important ways: God made us and God loves us. Listen to this story about how Jesus loved a woman** who was different from him.

One day, Jesus and his disciples traveled through the country of Samaria. Jesus and his disciples were Jews. The Jews didn't like the Samaritans because they were different. The Samaritans went to church in a different place than the Jews did, and they used a different Bible than the Jews did. The Jews hated the Samaritans so much that it was against the law to even talk to a Samaritan.

But, Jesus was kind to Samaritans. While Jesus and his disciples were traveling, they came to a town. They'd walked a long time and were hungry and thirsty. The disciples went to a town to buy some food, and Jesus sat down by a well to rest.

A Samaritan woman came to the well to get some water. Jesus was very thirsty, so he asked the woman to get him a drink.

The woman said, "I am surprised you're talking to me because you're a Jew and I'm a Samaritan."

Jesus said, "If you knew who I am, you'd ask for a drink of water that makes you live forever." Then Jesus told her that he's God's son and he brings life that never ends.

The Samaritan woman was so excited about Jesus that she went and told everyone she could find that Jesus was God's son.

Jesus cared so much about the woman and all the other Samaritans, he stayed with them for two days before continuing on his journey.

Ask:

● Is it ever hard to be kind to someone who's different from you?

● Has anyone ever been mean to you because of some way you're different?

● How did you feel when they were mean to you?

● What kind things can you do to make people who are different feel good?

Say: **You have some great ideas on how to be kind. We can be kind to everyone, even people who are different, because God is kind.**

5. Jesus Loves the Little Children

Sing "Jesus Loves the Little Children" with the kids in your class.

Say: **Even though we're all different in some ways, God made us all and he loves us all. Every one of us is precious to God.**

6. Pudding Paint

(You'll need paper and small bowls of prepared vanilla pudding colored with food coloring. You'll also need wet washcloths for cleaning up.)

Give children paper. Provide several small bowls of different-colored vanilla pudding. Have children finger-paint using several different colors of pudding.

As children are painting, ask:

● **What would it be like if all the pictures you made had to be exactly alike?**

● **What would it be like if all the people you knew looked exactly alike?**

Say: **We made beautiful pictures by mixing all these different colors. God mixes all kinds of people to make a beautiful world.**

Help children clean their hands, and set aside the pictures to dry.

7. A Fruity Snack

(You'll need exotic fruit, such as figs, papayas, mangoes, red bananas, mandarin oranges or pineapple. You'll also need paper cups, a pitcher of cold water and napkins.)

Serve the fruit with cups of clear, cold water. Say: **These are fruits that people in other countries eat every day.**

As children eat, talk about the kinds of food they eat every day.

8. Thanks for Differences

Close with the following prayer: **Thank you, God, for making us all different. We look different and we like different things. Thank you, God, for making us all the same. We all eat and we all like to have fun. And thank you for loving everyone just the way they are.**

by Mike and Amy Nappa

FRIENDS ARE KIND

By the time children get to kindergarten, they've learned to play *with* each other instead of *next* to each other. But they still need to develop friendship skills. These budding relationships need guidance to become the loving friendships God wants us to have.

Use this lesson to teach children that being kind is basic to friendship.

A POWERFUL PURPOSE

Kindergartners will learn to be kind.

A LOOK AT THE LESSON

1. If You Have a Friend and Know It (up to 5 minutes)
2. How to Be Kind (5 to 10 minutes)
3. Tear Art (5 to 10 minutes)
4. Freeze Tag (5 minutes)
5. Boaz Is Kind (up to 5 minutes)
6. Give a Grammy (up to 5 minutes)
7. A Songful Prayer (up to 5 minutes)

A SPRINKLING OF SUPPLIES

Gather glue, white paper, construction paper, a Bible, graham crackers, juice, paper cups and napkins.

THE LIVELY LESSON

1. If You Have a Friend and Know It

Sing "If You're Happy and You Know It" substituting the following words:

> **If you have a friend and know it, clap your hands.**
> **If you have a friend and know it, clap your hands.**
> **If you have a friend and know it, Let your kindness surely show it.**
> **If you have a friend and know it, clap your hands.**

Sing two more verses, substituting "stomp your feet" and "show a smile" for "clap your hands."

2. How to Be Kind

Say: **I'm glad we can be friends with e●ch other. The song we just sang told us to show kindness to our friends. A verse in the Bible talks about kindness. It says, "Be kind and loving to each other"** (Ephesians 4:32).

Ask:

● **What are some kind things we can do for our friends?**

Say: **Let's play pretend. I'll start a story. You can pretend that you're in the story. Each time I stop the story, think of all the kind things you could do.**

One day, a bunch of friends were playing in the sandbox. They built a castle. They piled up the sand and dug out the doors and windows. They shaped it into a beautiful castle. Everyone was having a good time until Matthew took the shovel away from Kimberly.

Ask:

● **What kind thing could you do?**

Say: **Next, they built a racetrack. They smoothed the sand and made turns and hills and valleys. Then they pretended to drive cars around the racetrack. Luis was just about to win the race when Jill accidentally fell and smashed the racetrack.**

Ask:

● **What kind thing could you do?**

Say: **Then they decided to dig a tunnel. They shoveled the sand until they made a great big mound in the middle of the sandbox. Then they dug and dug to make a tunnel through the pile of sand. They dug so quickly that some of the sand got in Kimberly's eyes.**

Ask:

● **What kind thing could you do?**

Then ask:

● **How did you feel when Matthew took the shovel away?**

● **How did you feel when Jill fell onto the racetrack?**

● **How did you feel when Kimberly got sand in her eyes?**

● **How did you feel when you thought of kind things you could do for them?**

Say: **Doing kind things for our friends makes them feel good and it makes us feel good, too.**

3. Tear Art

(You'll need glue, white paper and construction paper.)

Say: **One thing we can do to show kindness to friends is to give them something we've made. Let's make pictures. Then we can think of someone we'd like to give them to. It could be a friend in our families or any other friend.**

Give one child the glue; give one child enough white paper for everyone to have one sheet; and give the rest of the children each several sheets of construction paper. Tell kids to tear the construction paper into shapes and strips and glue them onto the white paper to make a colorful picture.

If they don't immediately figure out they need to share the supplies, say: **Show your kindness by sharing your supplies.**

As the children create their pictures, talk about the friend each child will give his or her picture to.

4. Freeze Tag

Say: **Let's play a game where we show kindness to one another.**

Play Freeze Tag for several minutes. Here are the rules: You will be "It" for the game. When you tag a child, he or she must freeze right there. Frozen children cannot move until a friend comes up and touches them, "unfreezing" them to continue play. Everyone must be kind and help one another out, or everyone will end up frozen.

After a few moments of play, gather kids in an open area and sit down.

Ask:

● **How did you feel when you were kind and "unfroze" a friend?**

● **How did you feel when someone unfroze you?**

If there were any children no one unfroze, ask:

● **How did you feel when no one unfroze you?**

Say: **It makes us feel good when we're kind and when others are kind to us.**

5. Boaz Is Kind

(You'll need a Bible.)

Open the Bible to the book of Ruth

and say: **There's a story in the Bible about a man who was very kind.**

Ruth and her mother-in-law, Naomi, moved to Judah during harvest time. They didn't have time to grow any grain, so they didn't have any food. So Ruth went to the fields one day to gather some of the grain that the field workers left behind.

Ruth worked hard to gather enough food for herself and Naomi. The sun was very hot, and Ruth got tired. But she only stopped a few minutes to rest.

The owner of the field, Boaz, noticed how hard Ruth was working. He told her to stay close to his workers and gather as much grain as she wanted. He even told his workers to drop some of the grain they harvested so it would be easy for Ruth to find.

When Ruth got thirsty, Boaz let her drink from the water jugs his workers had filled. And when she got hungry, he shared some of his workers' food with her. Boaz was kind to Ruth and made sure she had everything she needed.

6. Give a Grammy

(You'll need graham crackers, juice, paper cups and napkins.)

Say: **Let's get ready for a snack.**

Form two groups. Have one group of children stand against the left wall of the room and the other group stand against the right wall. Give the children on the left side of the room two graham crackers each. Tell them to wait to eat them. Give each child on the right side of the room two cups of juice. Ask them to wait to drink these, too.

Say: **Some of you have extra juice and some have extra crackers. Let's show kindness to each other by giving away part of what we have.**

Have the children walk to the center of the room and exchange the extra portions they were given with the people they meet in the middle.

Make sure you have extra treats in case kids don't share. It's not easy for children this age to think of the other person first. Don't force them to share if they're reluctant, but praise those who do share their treats.

7. A Songful Prayer

Sing this song as a closing prayer to the tune of "The Mulberry Bush":

Help us, God, to be kind to our friends,
Kind to our friends,
kind to our friends.
Help us, God, to be kind to our friends.
In every way we can.
          by Mike and Amy Nappa

PART 4:
A LIVELY LOOK
AT CELEBRATIONS

BIRTHDAY PARTY

Birthdays are important to children. They look forward to the celebration for weeks in advance. This lesson allows you to celebrate everyone's birthday with one big party, and it teaches kindergartners that God is helping them grow.

A POWERFUL PURPOSE

Kindergartners will see that God is helping them grow every day.

A LOOK AT THE LESSON

1. When I Grow Up (5 to 10 minutes)
2. Fill Their Shoes (5 to 10 minutes)
3. Samuel Grew (up to 5 minutes)
4. I'm Growing Every Day (up to 5 minutes)
5. Celebration Decoration (5 to 10 minutes)
6. Let's Sing "Happy Birthday" (up to 5 minutes)
7. A Birthday Feast (up to 5 minutes)
8. Thanks for Birthdays (up to 5 minutes)

A SPRINKLING OF SUPPLIES

Gather a box of dress-up clothes, a home center, a baby bootee, an athletic shoe, a Bible, balloons, tape, crepe paper streamers, colored paper, plastic sandwich bags, a birthday cake, candles, matches, a knife, plates, forks, punch and paper cups.

THE LIVELY LESSON

1. When I Grow Up

(You'll need a box of dress-up clothes and a home center. If your classroom doesn't have a home center, bring in old dishes, pots and pans. Use a classroom table for a dining room table. Paint four circles on a piece of plywood to make a stove. A plastic tub makes a great kitchen sink.)

As children arrive, have them put on one or two items from of the dress-up box. Then say: **Let's play grown-up. If you were a grown-up, what would you do?**

Have the class act out each child's suggestion. Children may suggest driving a car, going to work, mowing the lawn, reading the newspaper, cooking dinner, taking care of babies or cleaning the house.

Say: **You're not grown-ups yet, but you're growing. In a few years you'll be grown up because God is helping you to grow.**

2. Fill Their Shoes

(You'll need a baby bootee and an athletic shoe that a teenager might wear.)

Gather kids in a circle and sit down. Put the baby bootee in the middle of the circle. Say: **This is a shoe a baby wears.**

Ask:

● **What do babies do?**

Have kids act out what babies do.

They might cry, giggle, crawl or talk in baby talk.

Pick up the bootee and say: **All of you used to be babies and you used to do all of these things. But you've grown. Now you're in kindergarten. You don't act like babies anymore.**

Put the athletic shoe in the middle of the circle. Say: **This is a shoe a teenager wears.**

Ask:

● **What do teenagers do?**

Have kids act out what teenagers do. They might comb their hair, talk on the telephone, drive a car or do homework.

Pick up the shoe and say: **Someday you'll be teenagers and you'll do a lot of these things. God will help you grow bigger until you're teenagers.**

Have the children take off one of their own shoes and put it in the middle of the circle. Say: **These are shoes that kindergartners wear.**

Ask:

● **What do kindergartners do?**

Have kids act out what kindergartners do. They might play, run, jump, tie their shoes or pretend to write their names.

Say: **Right now you're kindergartners. You can do more things than babies can do, and soon you'll be able to do the things that teenagers do. God is helping you to grow every day.**

3. Samuel Grew

(You'll need a Bible.)

Open the Bible to 1 Samuel 1–3. Say: **Many years ago, a woman named Hannah wanted to have a baby. She prayed: "God, I am so sad because I don't have any children. Please give me a baby. If you do, I'll send him to the temple to serve you."**

God listened to Hannah's prayer, and soon she had a baby boy. She named him Samuel. When Samuel was old enough to eat solid food instead of baby food, Hannah took him to the temple to serve God.

Samuel lived with Eli, who was a leader in the temple. Eli took care of Samuel, and Samuel obeyed Eli and God.

Every year, Hannah made a coat for Samuel, and she traveled to the temple with Samuel's father to give it to him.

Every year, Samuel grew bigger and bigger. He did all he could to please God.

God was pleased with Samuel. When Samuel got bigger, God made him a messenger to the people.

Samuel grew just as you're growing. God watched over Samuel and helped him every day.

4. I'm Growing Every Day

While you read the following poem, lead children in acting it out. Start out curled up to make yourself as small as possible. Then grow and stretch as the poem indicates until you're standing on tiptoe with arms stretched above your head.

**When I was born,
I was very small.
Just a teeny, tiny baby.
But bit by bit and inch by inch,
God helps me to grow.
The games I play
and the food I eat,
Help me grow a little each day.
Right now, I am the perfect size,
To be in kindergarten.
But very soon, my bones
will stretch,**

**And I'll keep on growing
until I am,
The perfect size for a
grown-up person.**

5. Celebration Decoration

(You'll need blown-up balloons, tape, crepe paper streamers, colored paper and plastic sandwich bags.)

Say: **Every year on our birthdays, we celebrate getting bigger. Our birthdays are all on different days. But today, let's celebrate everyone's birthday with one big birthday party.**

Have kids decorate the room by taping balloons to the walls and putting up crepe paper streamers. Some children can make confetti by tearing colored paper into small pieces. Put the confetti in enough plastic sandwich bags for each child to have one.

6. Let's Sing "Happy Birthday"

(You'll need the bags of confetti.)

Hand out the confetti bags. Tell kids they're going to sing "Happy Birthday to You":

Happy birthday to you.

**Happy birthday to me.
Happy birthday to everyone.
Happy birthday to us.**

At the end of the song, have everyone throw their confetti.

After the lesson, have the children help pick up the confetti and put it back in their sandwich bags.

7. A Birthday Feast

(You'll need a birthday cake with candles, matches, a knife, plates, forks, punch and paper cups.)

Bring out the birthday cake and light the candles. Gather everyone around the cake and on the count of three, have all the children blow out the candles.

Cut and serve the cake. Pass out cups of punch. While you're eating the snack, have kids talk about what makes the best birthday celebration.

8. Thanks for Birthdays

Close with prayer, thanking God for the wonder of growth and the joy of birthdays.

by Kathy Downs

JESUS IS MY VALENTINE

Kindergartners use all their senses to understand what love is. To a kindergartner, love feels like hugs and kisses. It tastes like candy. It smells like cookies in the oven. It looks like Grandma. It sounds like a lullaby.

Use this lesson to teach kindergartners that God loves them and to show them ways to say, "I love you" to God.

A POWERFUL PURPOSE

Kindergartners will experience God's love and will express love for God.

A LOOK AT THE LESSON

1. Hide-and-Seek Hearts (up to 5 minutes)
2. God So Loved (up to 5 minutes)
3. What Is Love? (5 to 10 minutes)
4. I Love Jesus (up to 5 minutes)
5. Hearts of Love (8 to 10 minutes)
6. Heart Treats (up to 5 minutes)
7. Valentine Walk (5 to 10 minutes)

A SPRINKLING OF SUPPLIES

Gather red paper to photocopy the "Heart Tags" handout on, scissors, crayons, safety pins, a Nativity scene, red and pink construction paper, white paper, glue, markers, glitter, lace scraps, ribbon scraps, red Jell-O, knife or heart-shaped cookie cutter, juice, paper cups, napkins, a cassette player, music and tape.

THE LIVELY LESSON

1. Hide-and-Seek Hearts

(You'll need red paper, scissors, crayons and safety pins. Using red paper, photocopy and cut apart the hearts from the "Heart Tags" handout. Make enough for each child to have one heart. Hide the hearts around the room before class.)

Tell the children that valentines are hidden in the room. Have each child find one and write his or her name on the line. You may need to help them write their names. Then pin the valentines on each child as you would a nametag. As you pin the valentine, say: **God loves you, (Child's name).**

After everyone has a valentine pinned on, ask:

● **Who do we give valentines to?**
● **Why do we give valentines?**

Say: **We give valentines to show our love. God gave us a valentine, too. His name is Jesus.**

2. God So Loved

(You'll need a Nativity scene.)

Gather kids in a circle. Hand out a figure from the Nativity scene to each child. If you don't have enough figures, add toy animals. It's okay if they're out of proportion.

Have the kids tell the story of Jesus' birth. As they tell the story, have them arrange the Nativity scene in the middle of the circle.

If your kids aren't familiar enough

with the story to tell it without a lot of prompting, use this version: **God loved all the people in the world. He promised to send someone who'd love them and make a way for them to live with God forever.**

So God told Mary she was going to have a baby.

At the same time, the ruler of the country decided he needed to know how many people lived in his country. So he counted them all. Mary and Joseph went to Bethlehem to be counted. So many people came to Bethlehem that Mary and Joseph couldn't find a room to sleep in. They finally found a stable with many animals in it.

While they were there, Mary had her baby and named him Jesus. She wrapped him up and made a bed for him in a box that the animals usually ate out of.

Angels told some shepherds about the baby Jesus. So the shepherds traveled to Bethlehem to see him.

A bright star appeared in the sky. Wise men saw the star and followed it to where Jesus was. They brought presents for the baby.

When Jesus grew up, he loved the people just like God promised. He healed the sick people and took care of them. He taught the people about God. And he made a way for the people to live with God forever.

3. What Is Love?

Say: **Valentine's Day is a special day when we give valentines and say, "I love you." But the Bible says we should do loving things all the time. The Bible also says that** *every* **time we do a loving thing for someone we're really doing a loving thing for Jesus.**

Ask:
- **Who do you love?**
- **How does it feel to love that person?**

Have the children find partners by grabbing the hand of someone next to them. Say: **Let's practice doing loving things for our partners.** Pause after reading each of these pretend situations to let kids take turns doing these loving things for their partners:

Pretend your partner is thirsty. Get your partner a pretend drink.

Pretend your partner scraped a knee. Put a pretend bandage on the scrape.

Pretend it's your partner's birthday. Tell your partner what gift you'd give to him or her.

Pretend your partner has an itch on his or her back. Scratch your partner's back.

Pretend your partner is scared. Give your partner a hug.

Pretend your partner forgot to bring lunch. Share your pretend lunch with your partner.

Ask:
- **How did you feel when you did loving things for your partner?**
- **How did you feel when your partner did loving things for you?**
- **How do you think God feels when we're loving to each other?**

Say: **God is happy when we're loving to each other because it shows we love him.**

4. I Love Jesus

Teach kids this song to the tune of "Are You Sleeping?":

**Jesus loves me. Jesus loves me.
I love him. I love him.
I can do so much to
Show that I love Jesus.**

Yes, I can. Yes, I can.
I can tell him that I love him.
Yes, I can. Yes, I can.
I can do so much to
Show that I love Jesus.
Yes, I can. Yes, I can.

I can help my mom and dad.
Yes, I can. Yes, I can.
I can do so much to
Show that I love Jesus.
Yes, I can. Yes, I can.

I'll be kind to all my friends.
Yes, I will. Yes, I will.
I can do so much to
Show that I love Jesus.
Yes, I can. Yes, I can.

5. Hearts of Love

(You'll need small hearts cut from red and pink construction paper, white paper, glue, markers, glitter, lace scraps and ribbon scraps.)

Pile the small hearts in the middle of the table. Distribute white paper. Tell the children to take one heart for each person they love. If kids have trouble thinking of people, suggest parents, grandparents, brothers and sisters, neighbors, friends and God. Have the children glue their hearts to the paper and then decorate the paper with the markers, glitter, lace scraps and ribbon scraps.

While children are working, ask:
● **Who are your hearts for?**
● **Why do you love these people?**
● **What can you do to show these people that you love them?**

When children are finished, say:

Look at all the people we love. I'm glad you have so much love in your hearts. When we love people, we show God that we love him.

6. Heart Treats

(Follow the instructions for finger gelatin on the back of a package of red Jell-O. Cut the Jell-O into heart shapes. You'll also need juice, paper cups and napkins.)

Serve the Jell-O and juice. Pray: **Thank you, God, for showing your love for us by sending your son, Jesus. And thank you for giving us good food to eat.**

7. Valentine Walk

(You'll need a cassette player, music, markers, tape and as many sheets of paper as there are children in your class. Before class, draw a heart on one sheet of paper and draw happy faces on the rest. Tape the papers onto the floor in a circle.)

Say: **We're going to play Valentine Walk. While the music is playing, walk around the circle. When the music stops, stand on the sheet of paper nearest you.**

Play the music for a short period of time. When you stop the music, hug the child who's standing on the heart and pray: **Thank you, God, for loving (Child's name) so much that you sent Jesus to be (his or her) valentine.** Have the child sit inside the circle and clap with the music as you play the game again. Play until everyone has been hugged and prayed for.

by Kathy Downs

HEART TAGS

Photocopy and cut apart enough hearts for each child to have one.
Hide them in your classroom before the children arrive.

CELEBRATE JESUS

Kindergartners enjoy springtime. After staying inside so much during winter, they're ready for a lively celebration. This is a great time to share with kindergartners the good news about Jesus' resurrection. If you can, do this lesson outside. Nature holds many wonderful illustrations that'll help children understand the meaning of "new life."

Use this lesson to share with kindergartners the joy that comes from knowing that Jesus is alive.

A POWERFUL PURPOSE

Kindergartners will learn about the new life Jesus gives them.

A LOOK AT THE LESSON

1. The Bible Tells Me So (up to 5 minutes)
2. Butterflies (5 to 10 minutes)
3. Cocoons (up to 5 minutes)
4. Spring Flowers (up to 5 minutes)
5. God Gives Life (up to 5 minutes)
6. Jesus Is Alive! (up to 5 minutes)
7. Sing a Song of Good News (up to 5 minutes)
8. A New-Life Picture (up to 5 minutes)
9. Butterfly Snack (up to 5 minutes)

A SPRINKLING OF SUPPLIES

Gather a Bible, a highlighting marker, food coloring, small bowls of water, basket coffee filters, eyedroppers or pencils, pipe cleaners, cardboard tubes, brown construction paper, scissors, tape or glue, a marker, a flower bulb, a potted flower, a caterpillar (a real one, a toy, a picture or one made of cotton balls), napkins, carrot sticks, sandwiches, a knife, paper cups and juice.

THE LIVELY LESSON

1. The Bible Tells Me So

(Highlight Song of Solomon 2:11-12 in the Bible.)

Say: **The Bible tells us spring is a happy time. Listen to these Bible words.**

Show the children the highlighted words in the Bible. Read Song of Solomon 2:11-12 from the Bible or use the words printed below. Have kids join in doing the motions with you.

Winter is gone. (*Wrap arms around yourself and shiver*)

The rain has stopped. (*Raise arms above head and wiggle fingers while bringing arms down*)

Flowers are springing up. (*Squat down, then jump up*)

The time for (*point to watch or clock*)

The singing of birds (*flap arms, pretending they're wings*)

Has come. (*Motion with hand as if you're asking someone to come*)

Say: **Let's celebrate today. We can celebrate because spring reminds us that God has given us new life.**

2. Butterflies

(You'll need food coloring, small bowls of water, basket coffee filters, eyedroppers or pencils, and pipe cleaners.)

Say: **There are lots of butterflies during spring. Let's make butterflies to remind us of God's new life.**

Put several drops of food coloring in small bowls of water. Give each child a coffee filter. Have the kids make designs on the filters by sprinkling drops of colored water with the eyedroppers or pencils. Watch that children don't soak the filters with the colors. Wet filters tear more easily.

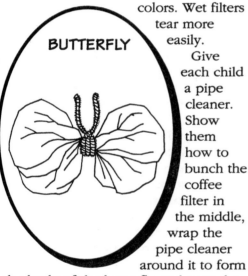

BUTTERFLY

Give each child a pipe cleaner. Show them how to bunch the coffee filter in the middle, wrap the pipe cleaner around it to form the body of the butterfly and twist the pipe cleaner to form the butterfly's antennae.

3. Cocoons

(You'll need cardboard tubes, such as paper towel tubes, toilet paper tubes or juice can tubes. You'll also need brown construction paper, scissors, tape or glue and a marker. Cut the construction paper into strips wide enough to fit around the tubes and 2 inches longer than the tubes.)

Say: **Butterflies come out of cocoons. Let's make cocoons for our butterflies.**

Give each child a cardboard tube and a strip of brown construction paper. Have kids wrap the construction paper around the tubes, leaving an inch of extra paper at both ends. Secure the paper with tape or glue. Then have kids gently crumple their butterflies and stuff them inside the cocoons. Have children push over the excess paper at both ends of the cocoons to close them like a roll of Life Savers. Write each child's name at the base of his or her cocoon.

COCOON

PAM

4. Spring Flowers

(You'll need a flower bulb and a potted, blooming spring flower such as a daffodil or tulip. Before class, hide the potted flower where kids can't see it.)

Show kids the flower bulb. Ask:

● **In the spring, this changes into something that looks very different from this—can you guess what it becomes?**

If no one knows, say: **This is a big flower seed called a bulb. In the spring, it grows to be a flower like this one.** Show kids the potted flower.

Ask:

● **If I wanted to make this big**

seed grow, what would I need to do?

● **Why does God make flowers and grass grow in the spring?**

Say: **One reason God made new things grow in the springtime is to help us remember that Jesus gives us new life. Let's learn a song about spring and the new life Jesus brings.**

5. God Gives Life

Teach this song and add your own motions. The tune is "Skip to My Lou."

Dig, dig, put in a seed.
Dig, dig, put in a seed.
Dig, dig, put in a seed.
Put seeds deep down in dirt.

Sprinkle, sprinkle here's
the rain.
Sprinkle, sprinkle here's
the rain.
Sprinkle, sprinkle here's
the rain.
It helps the seed to grow.

The sun comes out to warm
the dirt.
The sun comes out to warm
the dirt.
The sun comes out to warm
the dirt.
The flower soon will grow.

In springtime flowers start
to bloom.
In springtime flowers start
to bloom.
In springtime flowers start
to bloom.
God gives new life in spring.

Jesus rose to give us life.
Jesus rose to give us life.
Jesus rose to give us life.

New life he gives to us.

6. Jesus Is Alive!

(You'll need a Bible.)
Ask:

● **Have you ever known someone who died or had a pet that died?** Invite children to tell what happened. Be sensitive to children who may be grieving.

● **How did you feel?**
Open the Bible to Luke 24:1-9.

Say: **Jesus' friends felt very sad when Jesus died. Jesus spent many years teaching people and healing people. But one day he died. The friends of Jesus were sad when Jesus died because they thought they would never see him again. His body was placed in a cave. A large stone covered the doorway. Then something wonderful happened.**

Two days later, some women went to the cave where Jesus' body was. When they got there the big, heavy stone had been moved away from the doorway. They went inside the cave, but they couldn't find Jesus anywhere. When they came out of the cave, two men were there. The men said Jesus wasn't in the cave anymore because he was alive.

The women were so excited that they hurried to tell Jesus' friends they didn't have to be sad anymore because Jesus was alive.

Jesus is different from people we know who have died or pets that have died. People and pets don't come back to life on earth after they die even though people live in heaven after they die. But because Jesus is God, he came to life on earth again. That's why we celebrate Easter. Spring reminds us of

Easter because God makes the plants grow during spring.

7. Sing a Song of Good News

Say: **Here's a song that tells the good news.**

Teach this song to the tune of "Are You Sleeping?" Have kids march around the room while they sing the good news.

**Here is good news!
Here is good news!
Jesus lives! Jesus lives!
Now we all have new life.
Now we all have new life.
Praise the Lord! Praise the Lord!**

8. A New-Life Picture

(You'll need the cocoons with the butterflies in them that the children made earlier and a caterpillar. If you can't find a real caterpillar, a picture or a toy works just as well. Or, you can glue several cotton balls together and add legs and a face made of construction paper.)

Have the children get their cocoons and sit in an open area. Say: **Cocoons are a picture of the new life God gives us.**

Show the kids the caterpillar. Say: **A butterfly starts off like a caterpillar.**

Then it makes a cocoon, like the ones you made. The caterpillar hides inside the cocoon until it turns into a butterfly. Then it opens up the cocoon, climbs out, smooths its wings and flies away.

Have kids open up their cocoons, pull out their butterflies and smooth out the wings.

Say: **When we believe in Jesus, we become brand new—just like the butterfly is brand new. God gives us new life.**

9. Butterfly Snack

(You'll need napkins, carrot sticks, sandwiches cut diagonally, paper cups and juice.)

Pass out napkins, the carrot sticks and sandwiches.

Say: **Let's make a butterfly that we can eat. Put a carrot stick in the middle of your napkin. Then put half a sandwich on each side to look like wings. Now, let's thank God for the new life he gives the butterfly and for the new life Jesus gives us.**

Thank God for his gift of new life. Serve juice and enjoy the butterfly sandwiches.

by Kathy Downs

THANKS, GOD

Thanksgiving is recognized more for the food we eat and the television we watch than it is for giving thanks to a gracious God. Kindergartners may not understand why this holiday is important. They need to learn why we celebrate Thanksgiving.

Giving thanks is a natural response to God's love. Use this lesson to teach kindergartners to recognize God's gifts and to be thankful for them.

A POWERFUL PURPOSE

Kindergartners will learn that Thanksgiving is a time to say thank you to God.

A LOOK AT THE LESSON

1. Thanksgiving Dinner (5 to 10 minutes)
2. Only One Said Thank You (up to 5 minutes)
3. Sing a Song of Thanks (up to 5 minutes)
4. A Thankful Feast (5 to 10 minutes)
5. We Are Thankful (5 to 10 minutes)
6. A Thankful Parade (up to 5 minutes)
7. A Thankful Prayer (up to 5 minutes)

A SPRINKLING OF SUPPLIES

You'll need a home center. Gather a Bible, a popcorn popper, popcorn, candy corn, a bowl, napkins, juice, paper cups, construction paper, colored chalk, hair spray, tape and paper towel tubes, rulers or dowels. You'll also need a cassette player and a tape of praise music.

THE LIVELY LESSON

1. Thanksgiving Dinner

(You'll need a home center. If you don't have a home center in your classroom, bring in some plastic dishes and old pots and pans, paint four circles on a piece of plywood to make a stove and use a plastic tub for a sink. A classroom table makes a dining room table.)

Say: **Let's have a pretend Thanksgiving dinner.**

Have kids prepare and eat a pretend Thanksgiving meal in your classroom's home center. As they're working, ask questions such as "What does your family do for Thanksgiving?" "What do you eat at Thanksgiving?" and "Why do we have Thanksgiving?"

After the meal is eaten and the dishes are washed, say: **We have Thanksgiving to say thank you to God for all the things he gives us.**

2. Only One Said Thank You

(You'll need a Bible.)

Gather children in an open area. Open the Bible to Luke 17:11-19.

Ask:

● **Have you ever done something kind and no one said thank you?**

● **How did that make you feel?**

● **How do you feel when some-one says thank you to you?**

Tell this story: **One day, while Jesus was traveling to Jerusalem, he met 10 men who had a terrible skin disease. People were afraid of getting the disease so they made these 10 men live far away from all other people. The men were sad because in those days there wasn't a cure for the disease.**

When the 10 men saw Jesus, they hurried to ask him to heal them. Jesus told them to see the temple leaders. As the men started to go, they were healed.

One of the men rushed back to thank Jesus. But the nine other men didn't say thank you.

Ask:

● **How do you think Jesus felt when one man said thank you?**

● **How do you think Jesus felt when all the other men didn't say thank you?**

Say: **It makes everyone feel good when we say thank you.**

3. Sing a Song of Thanks

Say: **The Bible tells us to thank God because he is good. Let's sing a song of thanks to God.**

Sing this song with the children to the tune of "Praise Him, Praise Him":

**Thank him, thank him,
All you happy children,
God is good, God is good.**
(Repeat)

**Thank him, thank him,
All you happy children,
For your food, for your food.**
(Repeat)

Thank him, thank him,

**All you happy children,
For your homes, for your homes.**
(Repeat)

Ask children what they're thankful for. Create new verses of the song for each thing they mention.

4. A Thankful Feast

(You'll need a popcorn popper, popcorn, candy corn, a large bowl, napkins, juice and paper cups.)

Let the children help as much as possible in preparing the popcorn. While the corn is popping, say: **Thank you, God, this popcorn smells so good.**

Have children help mix the popcorn and the candy corn in a large bowl. Some children can help pass out the napkins and juice, while others pass out the treat. While children are working, say: **Thank you, God, that we can help each other.**

As you begin to eat, say: **Thank you, God, for this food. It tastes good and it fills us up.**

5. We Are Thankful

(You'll need construction paper, colored chalk, hair spray, tape and paper towel tubes, rulers or dowels.)

Say: **Let's make chalk pictures of things we're thankful for.**

As children draw, ask:

● **What are you thankful for?**

Spray the pictures with hair spray to keep the chalk from smearing. Help children tape their chalk pictures securely to paper towel tubes, rulers or dowels so they can wave them like flags. There should be enough tube left at the bottom for the child to hold.

6. A Thankful Parade

(You'll need the chalk-picture flags,

a cassette player and a tape of praise music.)

Have children march around the room while the praise music plays and wave their flags. Periodically, stop the music and ask:

● **What are you thankful for?**

Let two or three kids yell out what they're thankful for. Then start the music again. Continue until everyone has a chance to thank God.

Gather children in an open area. Ask:

● **How do you feel when you say thank you to God?**

● **How do you think God feels when you say thank you to him?**

7. A Thankful Prayer

Say: **God gives us so many good things. Let's thank him.**

On "go" have children run to something in the room they're thankful for. Pray: **We thank you, God, for . . .** and have kids each yell what they're thankful for.

Then have them choose something else they're thankful for and run there when you say "go." Say the prayer again.

Repeat several times. Then pray. **God, you have given us so many good things. We want to say thank you for all of them. Amen.**

by Kathy Downs

IT'S CHRISTMAS

For most kindergartners Christmas means getting toys. But it's never too early to begin emphasizing that the real reason we celebrate Christmas is because of Jesus' birth. Kindergartners need to know that even wise men from far away were full of joy when they found Jesus.

Use this lesson to help kindergartners understand the true meaning of Christmas.

A POWERFUL PURPOSE

Kindergartners will discover the joy the wise men felt when the special star they followed led them to a special baby—Jesus.

A LOOK AT THE LESSON

1. Wow! A Star Appeared (up to 5 minutes)
2. The Wise Men Followed (up to 5 minutes)
3. Twinkle, Twinkle, Special Star (up to 5 minutes)
4. A Special Apple-Star (5 to 10 minutes)
5. Pin the Star on the House (up to 5 minutes)
6. Starry, Starry Snack (up to 5 minutes)
7. Star Crowns (up to 5 minutes)
8. A Prayer of Thanks (up to 5 minutes)

A SPRINKLING OF SUPPLIES

Gather watercolors, paintbrushes, bowls of water, paint shirts, white paper, a white crayon, brown construction paper, tape, scissors, an aluminum foil pie pan, a flashlight, paper towels, tempera paint, flat pans, apples, a knife, a marker, wet washcloths, yellow construction paper, a blindfold, cream cheese, brown sugar, white sugar, vanilla, punch, paper cups and napkins.

THE LIVELY LESSON

1. Wow! A Star Appeared

(You'll need watercolors, paintbrushes, bowls of water and paint shirts. And for each child, you'll need a sheet of white paper on which you've drawn a star with a white crayon.)

Give each child a sheet of paper with a star on it. Say: **There is a surprise for you on this sheet of paper.**

Let the children discover the star by painting over the entire sheet of paper with the watercolor paint.

Ask:
● **What has appeared on your paper?**
● **What time of day do we see stars?**
● **What's fun about looking at stars?**

Say: **Once long ago, a very special star appeared in the sky.**

2. The Wise Men Followed

(You'll need two sheets of brown construction paper, tape, scissors, an aluminum foil pie pan and a flashlight. Tape one sheet of the brown construction paper to the wall lengthwise to form the main part of a house. Cut the other sheet diagonally, from one corner to another corner. Tape these two pieces to the wall to form a roof for your house. Before class poke several small holes in the

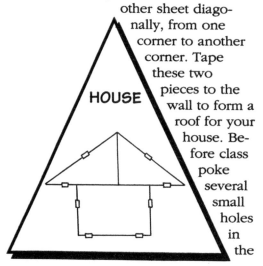

HOUSE

pie pan. They'll look like stars when you shine a flashlight through them.)

Darken the room. Shine the flashlight through the pie pan to make stars appear on the wall above the house.

Say: **One evening some wise and powerful men from the East saw a new star glittering far, far away in the heavens.** *(Poke a new, larger star in the pie pan)* **This star glowed with a bright light, brighter than any other stars in the sky, so they followed it.**

The star went ahead of them until it stopped over a little house. *(Move the stars down so the large star appears directly over the house)*

When they saw the star, they were very happy. The wise men went inside and found a baby. The baby's mother, Mary, held him close. When the wise men from the East saw this, they knelt down and worshiped the baby Jesus. They brought out gifts of gold, powder

that smells sweet when it's burned and sweet-smelling perfume. Gently, the men gave the baby their gifts. By following the new star, they found God's most special gift to us—the baby Jesus.

3. Twinkle, Twinkle, Special Star

Say: **God made the star shine so the wise men would find Jesus. God wanted the wise men to learn that Jesus is God's son. Jesus was born to show how much God loves us. We celebrate Christmas because it's Jesus' birthday.**

Sing the following song to the tune of "Twinkle, Twinkle, Little Star," and teach these actions to the children:

Twinkle, twinkle, special star,
(Hold your arm up high, and open and close your hand as though it were blinking)

God sent you to show the way,
(Place your right hand above your eyes as if you're looking at something far away)

For the wise men far away
(Pretend you're riding on a camel)

To the place where Jesus lay.
(Fold your arms and pretend to rock a baby)

Twinkle, twinkle, special star,
(Hold your arm up high, and open and close your hand as though it were blinking)

God sent you to show the way.
(Place your right hand above your eyes as if you're looking at something far away)

4. A Special Apple-Star

(You'll need white paper, scissors, paper towels, tempera paint, flat pans, paint shirts, apples, a knife, a marker and wet washcloths for cleaning up. Cut the paper into strips. The strips should be at least as wide as the apples are. You may need to tape or staple paper strips together so they're long enough to make headbands. Make "stamp pads" by putting several paper towels in flat pans and soaking the towels with thick tempera paint.)

Say: **I have another surprise for you.** *(Show kids an apple)* **There's something inside this apple that was in today's Bible story. What do think it is?**

Cut the apple in half. Instead of cutting from the top to the bottom of the apple, cut through the apple horizontally, halfway between the stem and the blossom end. Show kids the cut apple.

Ask:

● **What do you see?**

Say: **God has hidden a star in every apple.**

Cut enough apples so there is one half for each color of paint that you use. Show kids how to dip the cut side of the apple into the paint and stamp the paper strips. Let each child use the apple to stamp a paper strip. Write children's names on the strips and put them aside to dry.

5. Pin the Star on the House

(You'll need yellow construction paper, scissors, tape and a blindfold. Before class, cut a star for each child from the yellow construction paper. Put a tape loop on the back of each star.)

Ask:

● **Have you ever been lost?**

● **What was it like to be lost?**

● **How did you find your way again?**

Say: **It's easy to get lost when you don't know where you're going.**

Invite children to take turns putting on the blindfold and "pinning" a star on the house where the wise men found baby Jesus.

Ask:

● **Was it hard to find the house when you were blindfolded?**

● **What would've happened if a star hadn't shown the wise men where baby Jesus was?**

Say: **The wise men were glad God made the star shine because it kept them from getting lost. They were able to find the baby Jesus.**

6. Starry, Starry Snack

(You'll need fruit dip, apples, a knife, punch, paper cups and napkins. To make the fruit dip, blend 8 ounces of cream cheese with ¾ cup brown sugar, ¼ cup white sugar and a teaspoon of vanilla. Cut the apples horizontally into slices that show the stars inside.)

Serve the kids apple slices and punch. Let children dip their apple slices into the fruit dip.

Talk with kids about what their families do at Christmas.

7. Star Crowns

(You'll need tape and the paper strips stamped with apple-star prints.)

Distribute the paper strips and help kids tape the ends together to make headbands.

Say: **These headbands look like crowns full of stars. The wise men said that baby Jesus was a king. Your crowns will remind you that Christmas is the birthday of a king.**

8. A Prayer of Thanks

Close with prayer, thanking God for sending baby Jesus and for the special star that helped the wise men find him.

by Kathy Downs

CONTRIBUTORS

Patti Chromey works with children in her church in Pennsylvania.

Kathy Downs is Director of Children's Ministry at a church in Arizona.

Janel Kauffman teaches preschoolers and elementary-age children at a Christian school in Florida.

Amy Nappa is a freelance writer who lives in Loveland, Colorado.

Mike Nappa is Associate Editor for Group Books & Curriculum.

Eric Sandras is pursuing a Ph.D. in family education and has worked as a youth pastor.

Christine Yount is Editor for CHILDREN'S MINISTRY Magazine.

PRACTICAL HELP FOR CHILDREN'S MINISTRY

LIVELY BIBLE LESSONS

You can make creative teaching a snap with these 20 complete children's Bible lessons for each age level. Lively is better, because kids learn more. Each lesson has at least six child-size activities including easy-to-do crafts, action songs, attention-grabbing games, and snacks that reinforce the message. Plus, innovative new lessons are included to celebrate holidays like Valentine's Day, Easter, Thanksgiving, and Christmas. Just read the simple instructions, gather a few easy-to-find supplies, and you're ready to go!

Preschoolers
ISBN 1-55945-067-3

Grades K-3
ISBN 1-55945-074-6

Grades 1-2
ISBN 1-55945-098-3

FUN GROUP DEVOTIONS FOR CHILDREN'S MINISTRY

Use these 58 ready-to-go devotions to help your children grow closer to God. Each devotion has a theme, Bible passage, and fun learning experience where children use a variety of senses. Discussion questions help children understand how the devotion applies to their lives, and each devotion closes with a prayer. Devotion topics include...

- fear,
- anger,
- trust,
- gossip,
- success,

- jealousy,
- competition,
- friendship,
- God's love,
- self-worth,

- homework,
- obedience,
- promises,
- loneliness,
- embarrassment,

...plus holiday topics—Easter, Christmas, Thanksgiving—and more! Devotions are ideal for any setting where your children are gathered, such as...

- children's sermons,
- Sunday school,
- vacation Bible school,

- day camp,
- after-school programs,
- junior church.

ISBN 1-55945-161-0

Available at your local Christian bookstore. Or write:
Group Publishing, Inc., Box 485, Loveland, CO 80539.

INNOVATIVE RESOURCES FOR CHILDREN'S MINISTRY

MESSAGES FOR CHILDREN

Donald Hinchey

Captivate and challenge young listeners—with Bible-based sermons just for them. Each creative message uses language kids readily understand—so you'll teach meaningful lessons on topics such as...

- God's love,
- faith,
- putting God first,
- forgiveness,

...and dozens of other topics. Plus, each talk uses involving activities to grab and hold kids' attention—so they'll remember the truths you present.

You'll also get seasonal ideas for helping children understand the meaning of...

- Advent,
- Easter,
- Pentecost,
- Christmas,

...and other important days. You'll use these lessons for children's moments in Sunday worship—or at camps, retreats, and other special events.

5-Minute Messages for Children
ISBN 1-55945-030-4

6-Minute Messages for Children
ISBN 1-55945-170-X

ESTEEM BUILDERS FOR CHILDREN'S MINISTRY

Now Sunday school teachers have an effective new resource to help children from preschool through sixth grade learn to affirm and serve other children and adults. You'll get 101 esteem-building activities, including games, art projects, and service projects that will help children...

- develop their own positive self-image,
- understand how God views them as his creations,
- appreciate the God-given differences between people, and
- learn how to affirm others by their words and actions.

Each activity is easy to prepare; just gather a few easy-to-find supplies or photocopy one of the handouts included in the book. Makes a great opening exercise as children arrive in class.

ISBN 1-55945-174-2

Available at your local Christian bookstore. Or write:
Group Publishing, Inc., Box 485, Loveland, CO 80539.